Criticism of Labour Movement in 18th Century:

Perspectives in Marxism and Leninism

Dr.C.N. Baby Maheswari

Published by

Criticism of Labour Movement in 18th Century: Perspectives in Marxism and Leninism

ISBN 978-93-86638-02-1

Author

Dr.C.N. Baby Maheswari
Bonfring
309, 2nd Floor, 5th Street Extension, Gandhipuram,
Coimbatore-641 012.
Tamilnadu, India.
E-mail: info@bonfring.org
Website: www.bonfring.org
Phone: 0422 4213231

Dediction

Dedicated to

'MY TREASURE' DIVYA

and

DEEPAK

Preface

The role of literature and eminent writers, novelist of poet in the part of social movement (or) reform from social value (or) deadlock from civilized manner from the society in the particular venture. In this connection, the view (or) criticism of labor movement and paradigm shift on capitalistic approach to socialism (or) freedom from dictatorship method. Therefore, critical views and observation, narration on labor issues and practices and labour environment during 18th century. If, the pattern of life behavior and treatment with others (labours) were constant or peasant with human approach, it could have gone for discrimination of labor or violence against labor by capitalist. Instead, the existence of equality and solidarity where arouse.

In particular 18th &19th century labor movement was enormously emerged. After, Luyi-XIV assassination in France and '''Pastille " prison was demolished and devastated by general public due to labour victimized and the general people were cruelly suffered by monarchy.

In these days, how a poet, writers, and dramatists view on the labour movement in order to a paradigm shift for "Struggle against atrocity and domination by capitalist" either their views are seriously observed (or) leads any consequences and impact of sociological point of view. Any kind of inspiration where evolved from general public and rulers hand. Among the eminent literature, they described the nature, socio cultural aspects, ethnic in nature, political etc., but, the specific issue of labour and its movement on contemporary level was a meager level. During the 18th century, the labour movement was rigorous in the context of transitional changes from the larger traps with monarchy or autocratic rulers. It causes French revolution and industrial revolution.

Acknowledgement

Foremost, I would like to express my earnest gratitude to my university President Dr.ABULLAH AZIZ SUWAYYAN and Dr.ABDULLAH ALHARBI for having offered me with the opportunity.

I would like to extend my sincere thanks to my Dean Dr.REEM, Dean of Arts College Dr.FATIMAH MADHAANI for all their continuous support.

My heartfelt thanks goes to Dr.FADWA, Dr. AMAL, Ms.AREEJ and Ms.ABEER for their constant motivation and encouragement.

I would also like to extend my hearty thanks to my Friends and Colleagues for all their inputs and beneficial assistances.

I whole-heartedly thank my dearest Spouse, Mr.SEKAR NANJAYYAN MBA, MPhil, for all his understanding and love, for all his staggering support and for all that he has been which made my work a possible and a lot easier than it might otherwise have been.

I have no word to express how thankful I am to my daughter Dr.DIVYA KEERTHIKA and son Mr.DEEPAK SHABARISH. I am all I am today because of my children and I owe my success to their hardships, dedication and support. I also express my thanks to my Brothers and family for their support.

My special thanks to My Son-in-law and Daughter-in- law for being my moral support at all times of my life. Last but not least, I profoundly thank my most adorable Grandsons my dearest SHASRRIK and ADHVIK who loves me like none other.

CHAPTER - I

Introduction

The renaissance of the labor movement and transitional changes were begun from the 18th century. The exploitation and discrimination a domination were led by capitalist and dictatorship or monarchy rulers. Because of, the bottleneck and carnage of labour environment were brutally engaged in 17th centuries before that the writers and dramatist were narrated or described the topics in which metaphor of natural things, imagination and compression with epics. Ex: William shake sphere who famous and biggest name in the specialized field of drama. Similarly, Ben Johnson, who belonged to dramatist and poet where famous for satirical stage productions that illuminated human flaws via darkly comedic plots. Next to John Milton, who belonged to writer and dramatist where there was an epic by Homeric style (homers) thus, all kinds of literature shown the criticism and comparison for natural recourse civilization, emperor's life style and ruling style, behavioral approach, historical movement. After the 16th century (shake spears contemporaries).

The literature movement and its significance (criticism) were transformed or paradigm shift to bourgeois and capitalist movement. The major part or core areas of description were sociological and cultural aspects of working class groups. A very few of writers and poets were criticized about the transitional changes and practices of the labour environment during the revolutionary period, even though major changes have been made in this scenario, the movement (labour) is a dynamic one. In means a large number of people (labour) who pushed into the capitalistic approach after 1990 in the context of globalization. It emerges global network of labour movement with international policy programs were entertained. These changes have emerged a large number of international migration (labour) and transformation of chapters well expressed the view and narration of writes (or) poets (or) novelist's criticism and narration about the political view, labor market, capitalism, the working class, social integration transitional changes of the labour movement from revolutionary period to globalized era.

The Industrial Revolution-Interpretations from 1830

Industrial Revolution: a rapid development in industry. The development which took place in England in the late eighteenth and early nineteenth centuries, chiefly owing to the introduction of new or improved machinery and large-scale production methods (Oxford English Dictionary).

Whilst few have disputed that the world's first 'industrial revolution' took place in Britain, that expression. The 'Industrial Revolution' was not a British invention. The precise roots of the term are unclear, but it seems to have been coined in France in the early nineteenth century, by political economists struck by the tremendous economic and social advances that had recently been made across the Channel. A revolution industrial had occurred, they declared, an economic counterpart to the political revolution franchise that had occurred at home half a century earlier, with social consequences every bit as far reaching. In the first few decades of the nineteenth century, the expression 'revolution industrial' became firmly rooted in the French language, and although it was deployed somewhat loosely, it nonetheless had a meaning clearly recognizable today: namely significant economic growth achieved through the use of new technology and machines.(JJ.Fazy) By the second half of the nineteenth century, French commentators were debating the extent to which a French, rather than British, industrial revolution had occurred, and writers from the provinces were starting to write about the industrial revolutions that were taking place in their parts. In the overwhelmingly rural region of Brittany, a commentator at the end of the century thought he could discern the germ of an evolution rather than a revolution industrial, but was forced to concede that even that was proceeding 'lentement Whilst the linguistic origins of the 'industrial revolution' doubtless lie in France, it was a German writer, the great Prussian philosopher, Friedrich Engels, who developed the meaning of the expression most fully. 'Die industrial Revolution' was a pivotal event in Engel's monumental study of the laboring poor in Manchester – The Condition of the Working Classes in England – signifying a crucial period of transition in British history. For Engels the industrial revolution was the culmination of a series of technical improvements in the textiles industry, small improvements individually but collectively giving rise to profound and far-reaching change. The process started with James Hargreaves' spinning jenny, invented in 1764. Engels explained This invention made it possible to deliver more yarn than heretofore.

Whereas, though one weaver had employed three spinners, there had never been enough yarn, and the weaver had often been obliged to wait for it, there was now more yarn to be had than could be woven by the available worker. Now that the weaver could earn more at his loom, he gradually abandoned his farming, and gave his whole time to weaving... By degrees the class of farming weavers wholly disappeared, and was merged in the newly arising class of weavers who lived wholly upon wages, had no property whatever ... and so became working men, proletarians.

This process was accelerated by a series of subsequent inventions. The spinning jenny was quickly followed by Richards Arkwright's spinning throttle and carding engine, Crompton's mule, Cartwright's power loom, and James Watt's steam-engine, and this succession of inventions led in turn to the industrial revolution – 'the victory of machine-work over hand-work Like contemporaneous French writers, Engels both highlighted both the transformative role played by new machinery and drew parallels between England's and France's very different revolutions. 'The industrial revolution,' he wrote, 'is of the same importance for England as the political revolution for France. The differentiate between England in 1760 and in 1844 is at least as great as that between France under the ancient régime and during the revolution of July'. But the character the Engels' industrial revolution was also quite different from that of French intellectuals, owing to the emphasis he placed upon the emergence of a new class of landless workers with nothing to their name but the wages they were able to earn by their own labour. This was, he argued, 'a revolution which altered the whole civil society'. Admittedly, this account of 'revolution' within British society was built upon a somewhat rosy description of life for the workers prior to mechanization – according to Engels, they had lived 'a passably comfortable existence, leading a righteous and peaceful life in all piety and probity'. Nonetheless, Engels' account amounted to a complete interpretation of the British industrial revolution, emphasizing the transformative role played by technology .But the influence of Engels on mid-nineteenth-century conceptions of industrialization was in fact extremely limited. Though his work, in time, has cast a very long shadow over interpretations of the industrial revolution, and of its social consequences in particular, it initially had little impact in Britain. None of his work was translated from the German until the 1880s, and until that date, was largely passed over by British political economists and social commentators, who remained blissfully unaware of their industrial revolution and newly created industrial proletariat.

So , French and German commentators became increasingly confident in their use of the term 'industrial revolution', in England, where this revolution was widely believed to have occurred first, the concept was slow to take root. It was not until the 1840s that the expression began to filter into the English language, and its meaning when it did so was unsettled. The term was picked up and used by a few British economists in much the same sense as their French colleagues. The political economist Sir Travers Twiss, for example, declared that at the same time as the 'great social experiments, to which the Political Revolution of France had given rise to on the continent .An industrial revolution was silently operating in England, leading to results still more remarkable'.(Travers Twiss-London)

At the same time, John Stuart Mill referred to the possibility that the opening of foreign trade might usher in an 'industrial revolution' in a country 'whose resources were previously undeveloped for want of energy or ambition in the people'. (John Stuart Mill) But whilst some use of the expression in the English language can certainly be detected, it is also fair to conclude that it was used only occasionally and without much consistency. Through most of the nineteenth century, British commentators preferred to speak of manufactures rather than industry, and of progression and advance, rather than revolutions. By the middle of the century, the expression had largely dropped out of the language. Political economists and social commentators managed to make sense of dramatic recent economic and industrial developments without recourse to the special phrase coined by their European neighbours. As early as 1814, Patrick Colquhoun found it 'impossible to contemplate the progress of manufactures in Great Britain within the last thirty years without wonder and astonishment. Its rapidity exceeds all credibility', and over the next few decades similar sentiments were echoed over and over again by all those with any interest in Britain's economic growth.(P. Colquhoun). In line with most European commentary, discussions of Britain's growing economy tended to focus upon invention, machinery, and factories. For example, Andrew Ure, the Scottish chemist turned social commentator, declared in his Philosohy of Manufactures, published in 1835: 'This island is pre-eminent among civilized nations for the prodigious development of its factory wealth'. The spectacularly successful Great Exhibition, held in the newly erected Crystal Palace in Hyde Park, London, epitomized this widely held sense of progress and achievement. The tens of thousands of arte facts, displayed by 14,000 exhibitors from 28 different countries testified both to the nation, and to the world, the exceptionally productive and sophisticated nature of the British economy.(John Robert Gold & Margaret M. Gold).

In 1851, Britain was undoubtedly the richest nation in the world: both its economy and population were growing rapidly, and it had the largest and most technologically advanced manufacturing sector. This, then, was not a nation unaware of the profound economic changes that had been wrought in its recent history; it was indeed in no doubt that the rapid growth in manufactures in recent decades marked an epochal moment in British history. The Victorians simply did not turn to the metaphor of revolution in order to understand these developments. It was not until the end of the nineteenth century, with the work of the social reformer and historian, Arthur Toynbee, that the term an 'industrial revolution' decisively entered the English language. Toynbee's lectures, originally delivered to Oxford undergraduates between October 1881 and May 1882 under the title 'On the economic history of England, 1760-1840' were re-titled Lectures on the Industrial Revolution in England for publication. They proved immensely popular, going through no fewer than five editions in the following two decades and remaining in print until 1927.(D.C. Coleman) Nor was the substitution of the words 'industrial revolution' at the moment of publication merely accidental; the idea of 'revolution' lay at the heart of Toynbee's book. In his view, the period 1760-1840 marked a fundamental transformation of the English economy, comprehending changes in population, agriculture and industry, as well as in the social lives of the poor. The 'essence of the industrial revolution', he concluded, was the replacement of medieval guilds and regulation with capitalist competition. (Arnold Toynbee)

In emphasizing that industrialization brought in its wake a number of deleterious consequences for the laboring poor, Toynbee shared considerable common ground with Engels, though there is no evidence that he had ever read Engels', as yet untranslated, Condition of the Working Classes.(Coleman) Within a few decades the expression had entered the vocabulary of historians, undergraduates, and even members of the chattering classes and workers' educational movements. The industrial revolution was a pivotal concept, for example, in the immensely popular works of John and Barbara Hammond, read widely both within and without the academy.(J. L. Hammond and Barbara Hammond) Although the language of revolution had not seemed apposite to those living through the unprecedented industrial change of the late eighteenth and early nineteenth centuries, for the following generation, looking at the same events at the remove of several decades, the metaphor of revolution was compelling.

But no sooner had the newly re-found expression began to gain a degree of popular currency, than the academic community began to question the existence of this supposed 'industrial revolution'. In the early twentieth century, a new generation of scholars began questioning whether the industrial revolution was so 'revolutionary', or indeed so located in 'industry', as the ebullient Toynbee had declared, and many avoided using the term altogether. The critique came from both theorists and historians. The influential economist Joseph Schumpeter, writing prolifically through the 1920s and 1930s, emphasized long cyclical movements in economic history rather than turning points and watersheds. His ideas were most clearly expressed in his 1942 work, Capitalism, Socialism, and Democracy, where he wrote of the 'long waves of economic activity... Each of them consists of an "industrial revolution".(Joseph Schumpeter) In Britain he perceived no fewer than five 'industrial revolutions', and placed the classic period of Toynbee's industrial revolution 'on a par with at least two similar events which preceded it and at least two more which followed it. Their critique rested upon a reassessment of the pace and extent to which any British industries were revolutionized. H. Heaton, for example, drew attention to the long term origins of change and to the slow duration of industrialization once it actually begun, declaring that a revolution taking so long to occur 'may well seem to need a new label'.(Pat Hudson) Sir John Clap ham, writing from the distinguished position of a chair in economic history at the University of Cambridge, noted that even the cotton industry was only partially revolutionized by 1850, whilst whole sectors of the economy remained virtually unchanged. He observed that in 1850, fully half of the population was still employed in areas wholly untouched by industrialisation. (J. H. Clapham)The emphasis was firmly on the gradual rather than revolutionary nature of nineteenth-century economic change. At the same time as historians of eighteenth- and nineteenth-century Britain played down the extent and pace of economic change during that period, specialists in other periods were busy identifying new 'industrial revolutions' of their own. So, for example, E. M. Carus-Wilson argued that innovations to the fulling mill in the thirteenth century amounted to an 'industrial revolution which destined to alter the face of medieval England'. (E. M. Carus-Wilson)

John Nef's researches on the coal industry led him to conclude that an 'industrial revolution' had occurred there in the century between 1540 and 1640.(J. U. Nef) He later expanded this theory into a broader account of technological change throughout the economy in the century after 1540. The developments he discerned in this period were so striking, it led him to reject the eighteenth-century historians' claim to an 'industrial revolution': 'the concept of an "industrial revolution"', he argued, 'would seem to be especially inappropriate as an explanation of the triumph of industrial civilization in Great Britain. It gives the impression that the process was especially sudden, when it was in all probability more continuous than in any other country'. (J. U. Nef)Though not all writers followed Nef in dismissing the concept of an eighteenth-century industrial revolution, these contributions by scholars working outside the traditional time-frame of industrialization, certainly helped to provide a fundamental revision of the concept that Toynbee had developed. In some ways it marked a return to the 'industrial revolution' employed by some French writers a century earlier – a rapid advance, usually led by technological change, but in just one industry, one place, or at one time, rather than a single, national event, a more fundamental reorganization of an entire economy. Historians therefore spoke of industrial revolutions rather than industrial revolution and of an extensive and piecemeal process of change rather than of an intensive and transformative one. It is interesting to note that this reinterpretation of the extent and significance of the industrial revolution occurred at a time that the British economy was generally in the doldrums and

Britain's relative decline to other industrial nations was unmistakable. Perhaps from this perspective of economic slowdown, it seemed more apposite to view Britain's economic success between 1750 and 1850 as part of a much larger cycle of rise and fall of different nations' economy rather than as a transformative and uniquely British event. Yet the writing of history rarely stands still. No sooner had scholars shaped a process of gradual and piecemeal industrialization, then interpretative fashions changed once again, and the fast-paced 'revolution' that Toynbee had postulated, seemed to be back in vogue once more. Once again, both theorists and historians seemed to speak a shared language, identifying a relatively short, and certainly dramatic, event occurring on a national stage – not to be confused with local revolutions or piecemeal revolutions in single industries. The Yale-educated economic theorist Walt Rostov's The Stages of Economic Growth was hugely influential on post-war conceptions of industrialization. Rostov not only held that an industrial revolution, the world's first, had occurred in Britain somewhere between 1790 and 1850, but even argued that it represented the lynchpin of modern history: the economic step-change that all nations had to emulate in order to thrive. Rostov defined the industrial revolution as a period of rapid economic growth, or 'take off' – he dated 'take-off' in Britain between 1783 and 1802 – followed by sustained higher levels of economic growth. (Walt Whitman Rostov) This model formed a sharp contrast to Schumpeter's account of long patterns of cyclical growth. Here was an altogether punchier story, with the industrial revolution marking a watershed in not just British but in world history. His account was not of course simply swallowed wholesale by British economic historians, but it did seem to provide them with a meaningful framework for the study of industrialization, and in the years that followed, the focus switched from downplaying the significance of change during the period to identifying the moment of 'take-off'. The most influential work in this vein was produced by the economic historians Phyllis Deane and W. A. Cole, who returned to the economic records collected at the time in order to provide groundbreaking estimates for the size and rate of growth of the economy between the late seventeenth and mid-twentieth century's. Whilst considering the concept of take-off to be a 'dramatic simplification' and taking great care to stress the deep roots of economic change, Deane and Cole nonetheless spoke of a 'crucial breakthrough', and it was this theme that seemed to resonate most widely amongst scholars. (Phyllis Deane)Throughout the 1960s and 1970s, the existence of an 'industrial revolution' was widely held as an article of faith. One of the leading historians of the 1960s, Eric Hobsbawm, saw fit to declare that the `Industrial Revolution marks the most fundamental transformation of human life in the history of the world recorded in written document'.(Eric Hobsbawm)

Elsewhere, the nation's pre-eminent historians spoke of 'one of the great watersheds in the history of human society'; a 'great upheaval'; and a 'great discontinuity'. (M.W. Flinn & Hartwell, R.M). It all amounted to a total revision of the pre-war generation's account of industrialization. Nor was this new account of the rapidity of economic growth between the late eighteenth and middle of the nineteenth centuries confined to the pages of economic history textbooks and journals. This great watershed in the economic sphere was presumed to have spilled over from the economic to the social, transforming wide areas of social life as it did so. For example, Edward Thompson's seminal account of the formation of the 'working class' was predicated upon the existence of widespread mechanization and the rise of the factory. (E. P. Thompson)

The emergence of Chartism and other working-class political movements was explained in terms of the dramatic-and largely pernicious–industrial revolution that workers were forced to live through.(John Foster) Even areas of cultural, personal and recreational life, topics that might appear largely unconnected with the worlds of industry and work, were interpreted against the backdrop of a rapid and deep-rooted industrial revolution. Thus studies of religion, for example, sought to link a presumed decline in religious belief with the rise of the factories and cities.(Alan D. Gilbert) Research into family life debated the thesis that the rise of the cotton industry and technological changes in work organization created crisis in family relations.(N.J. Smelser) Even patterns of recreation were left permanently altered by industrialization. According to Robert Malcolmson, popular sports and pastimes were first undermined and finally destroyed by the industrial revolution, leaving a vacuum in place of the rigorous recreational calendar that had existed in the eighteenth century. (R. Malcomson) There was, endless disagreement amongst historians over the fine details of change in all of these areas, yet most were working within a recognizably shared framework. These interpretations of social and cultural life were embedded in a cataclysmic interpretation of the period. For two full decades, the focus was on the dramatic social change ushered in by the world's first industrial revolution, which was now clearly identified as a momentous turning point in both economic and social life. Once again, it is interesting to note the contemporary social and economic context for these interpretations of the industrial revolution. This dramatic reinterpretation of industrialisation occurred at a time of sustained economic growth in western Capitalist economies. Post-war reconstruction with its record levels of investment, near full employment, and new public services such as subsidized housing, free health care, and improved access to secondary schooling and university education, had ushered in an undeniable rise in western living standards. It also made apparent the very stark difference between the prosperous industrialised west and the impoverished, non-industrialised 'Third World'. For scholars writing in the 1970s, it no longer seemed appropriate to relegate British economic growth around the turn of the eighteenth century to the status of just another economic upturn, a glorious, but ultimately short-lived, moment of triumph in the British economy. From this perspective, it appeared to mark a much more significant turning point in the transition to modern society.(Cannadine) But as should already be abundantly clear, historical interpretations rarely stand still for long, and so proved the case for this dramatic account of industrialisation. No sooner had the ink dried on the latest accounts of the revolutionary social changes wrought by industrialisation, than a new challenge to the concept was made–issuing, once again, from those presumed to know best in such matters: the economist historians. In the late 1970s, E.A. Musson's textbook on the Growth of British Industry declared that the notion of a short and cataclysmic industrial revolution was 'clearly no longer tenable'(A.E. Musson). This account was led further, highly influential, support in the 1980s by a new breed of economic historians, preoccupied with measuring the various indicators of national economic growth–growth in industrial output, gross domestic product, productivity, and so forth–and armed with an impressive command of economic theory and complex statistical methods. First Knick Harley provided a critique of Deane and Cole's estimates for economic growth, suggesting they had over-estimated growth during the crucial years 1770-1815.(C. Knick Harley)The revision was completed shortly after by Nick Crafts, an economist based in Oxford, who reworked growth rates in the period 1970-1830 indicating much slower growth than the concept of rapid take-off permitted.

This research inevitably had a profound impact on the existing literature, for by this point the industrial revolution was not simply an economic event, but it also, to quote Hobsbawm once more, 'the most fundamental transformation of human life in the history of the world'. In fact,if there had been no dramatic economic revolution, where did this leave all those social transformations, watersheds, and discontinuities that two decades of social, as well as economic, history had described? As ever, reinterpretation of the economic sphere spilled into the social, and this revision to the dramatic interpretation of the period 1760-1850 that dominated both economic and social histories raised a certain degree of alarm amongst the historical profession. Patrick O'Brien observed that 'the British Industrial Revolution is once again under attack as a "misnomer", a "myth" and dismissed as one among a "spurious list of revolutions". (Patrick K. O'Brien) And in their highly influential response to Crafts' work, Maxine Berg and Pat Hudson declared that 'the notion of industrial revolution has been dethroned almost entirely'.(Maxine Berg and Pat Hudson) But the consequences of these new estimates for economic growth were more complicated than the notion of a 'dethroning' of the industrial revolution admits. It is certainly true that one or two maverick voices questioned the use of the term, but in reality one needs to search the literature long and hard to find scholars who used Crafts' new statistics to argue that the concept of an industrial revolution was no longer valid.(J. C. D. Clark) In fact, what Crafts did was not dethrone the industrial revolution, but force scholars to question more deeply what exactly the 'industrial revolution' was. It was a problem with no easy answers, and we are arguably still witnessing the full unfolding of responses to this question. The historians' initial response was to challenge the validity of this new set of statistics. A number of historians picked over the records Crafts had exploited, the assumptions he had made, and the methods he had used. By looking in detail at every element of these figures, critics sought to demonstrate not only that Crafts' figures were subject to a considerable margin or error, but also that many of these errors were likely to underestimate, rather than exaggerate, the overall rate of growth. We will review both Crafts' figures, and these criticisms, more fully in the chapter that follows, for the present, however, it is important to note that this critique ultimately resulted in a modification, rather than an outright rejection, of the new estimates provided. For all the dissatisfaction that historians expressed with the new estimates, there was no desire to return to the older idea of short period of dramatic economic growth. Instead, within less than a decade, it was clear that most economic historians begrudgingly accepted that during the classic period of the industrial revolution, economic growth, if not quite so slow as Crafts argued, was none the less considerably slower than an earlier generation had imagined. But for most historians evidence of slow economic growth simply did not provide compelling grounds for dismissing the concept of an industrial revolution. The general consensus was that growth rates were no way to measure the existence (or otherwise) of a phenomenon so complex as the industrial revolution. In this line of argument, the growth rates are not so much inaccurate as simply irrelevant, since they measured phenomena that had little do with the industrial revolution. Yet in pursuing this line of argument the ground between Crafts and his critics was much less than was sometimes implied. Though Crafts never described his figures as 'irrelevant', he certainly did use them to argue it was time to redefine the 'industrial revolution'. Crafts found evidence of both slow national growth and a significant restructuring of the workforce – marked above all by the transfer of workers from agriculture to new industrial occupations – a restructuring that he considered to be amply sufficient to justify the continued use of the term 'industrial revolution'. In the event, this alternative definition of the industrial revolution offered by Crafts received very much less attention than his statistics had. With a newly shared consensus that national growth rates were not pivotal to understanding the industrial revolution, the ground was leveled for new interpretations and assessments. Specialists of different areas of the early industrial economy were quick to re-emphasize the significance of their particular area of interest The role of inventions, for example, once again received critical attention. New technologies of course had long held a central position in interpretations of the industrial revolution. They had lain at the heart of French and German definitions of the industrial revolution in the nineteenth century, and had also been integral to English uses of the expression, once it became commonplace in the early twentieth century. Maxine Berg focused attention on areas of the industrial economy that had traditionally received rather little attention: the worlds of female and child labour, of domestic work and artisan workshops, handheld tools, small machines, and skilled labour–what she called 'the other Industrial Revolution'.(Maxine Berg) Despite looking beyond the steam engines and factories that long formed the mainstay of industrial history, Berg found evidence of a 'transformation of production processes and regions... and restructuring of industry over the course of the eighteenth and nineteenth centuries', and was left in no doubt that these changes this amounted to an industrial revolution. Meanwhile, Tony Wrigley placed critical emphasis on the emergence of a new source of fuel, coal. Prior to the industrial revolution the economy was dependent upon the power provided by wood, wind, water, horses, and humans, and only limited growth was achievable by these means. Power provided by the wind was unreliable and water power could only be provided by fast-flowing rivers, which effectively restricted its use to a finite number of locations. The power provided by horses and wood could be more actively expanded, but increasing power from either of these sources required land, either to grow the fodder for the horses, or to grow woodlands to provide the timber. Yet, as Wrigley points out, the landmass of Britain was fixed, so extending the amount of land to be put to industrial purposes effectively required taking it out of cultivation for human consumption, and that in turn would restrict the possibilities of demographic growth. Therefore, we could have either industrial growth or population growth: you could not have both. Yet we know that at some point during the period 1700-1850, Britain entered a new era of sustained economic growth combined with population growth, breaking free from this centuries' old pattern of limited growth. According to Wrigley, the switch to coal provides the key to understanding this process. Switching to coal tapped a massive new source of energy that enabled industry to grow to a previously unimaginable extent, growth moreover which did not occur at the expense of feeding and housing the population. This process, he argued, provides the key to understanding the British industrial revolution.(E. A. Wrigley)

Most analyses of the British industrial revolution have tended to look at supply to focus upon how improvements in technology or increases in capital, energy, or raw material enabled the economy to grow. In a departure from this tradition, Jan de Vries has argued that it is necessary to consider rising demand along side changes in supply in order to understand British industrialisation.(J. De Vries) According to de Varies, this rise in demand stemmed from a twofold change in the way in which families earned and spent their income. Firstly, workers had traditionally exhibited a preference for leisure over goods, that is, they had worked just so long as was necessary in order to procure life's essentials – housing, food and clothing – and then abandoned work (and the possibility of buying small luxuries with those extra wages) for leisure. In the second half of the seventeenth century, this traditional working pattern gave way to a more recognisably 'modern' pattern, in which individuals worked longer hours in order to earn the wherewithal to purchase a few luxuries – tea, sugar, new cotton clothing, a decorative plate, or whatever else the consumer desired. Secondly, early modern workers had tended to produce much of what they consumed within the home rather than buying it at the market place: so a household got by by growing a few potatoes in the garden, baking their own bread, brewing their own beer, and making their own clothes – cheaper alternatives to buying such goods and services from others. At the same time as families began to work harder in order to purchase small consumer goods, they also abandoned this domestic production in favor of buying goods readymade at the market, or even in one of the nation's rapidly growing number of shops. Although this change in household behavior proceeded slowly, it gradually led to a rise in demand over the eighteenth century, which helped in turn to stimulate industrial growth. It constituted, de Varies argued, an '"industrious revolution"... which preceded and prepared the way for the industrial revolution'.(Hans-Joachim)

As ever, it is interesting to probe the social and economic context within which historians provided these interpretations of the industrial revolution. Historians began to criticize the dramatic interpretation of the industrial revolution at the end of the 1970s; their critique emerged at the end of the unparalleled growth and prosperity of the post-war years and coincided with high inflation, high levels of unemployment and considerable social and economic discontent. At the same time, however, Britain's economic difficulties in the 1970s could be readily understood as just one of the economic downturns that a free market economy was sure to experience periodically, and whilst the nation's decline relative to other industrial neighbors was likely to continue, the continuation of absolute growth and rising living standards was not thrown into doubt. The difference between those countries that had undergone industrialization and those that had yet to do so remained as clear as it had done twenty years earlier, and this economic slowdown did not call for a fundamental rethink of the world's first industrial revolution. The parallels between the historians' own times and their accounts of British industrialization was noted a quarter of a century ago by the historian David Canadian: 'each generation of economic historians,' he observed, 'has evolved a dominant interpretation of the Industrial Revolution which bears so strong an affinity with contemporary circumstances that it cannot be merely accidental'.(Canadian)

Labour Movement in Revolutionary Period

Early Industry

Early 18th century British industries were generally small scale and relatively unsophisticated. Most textile production, for example, was centered on small workshops or in the homes of spinners, weavers and dyers: a literal 'cottage industry' that involved thousands of individual manufacturers. Such small-scale production was also a feature of most other industries, with different regions specializing in different products: metal production in the Midlands, for example, and coal mining in the North-East. New techniques and technologies in agriculture paved the wave for change. Increasing amounts of food were produced over the century, ensuring that enough was available to meet the needs of the ever-growing population. A surplus of cheap agricultural labour led to severe unemployment and rising poverty in many rural areas. As a result, many people left the countryside to find work in towns and cities. So the scene was set for a large-scale, labour intensive factory system.

Steam and Coal

Because there were limited sources of power, industrial development during the early 1700s was initially slow. Textile mills, heavy machinery and the pumping of coal mines all depended heavily on old technologies of power: waterwheels, windmills and horsepower were usually the only sources available.

Changes in steam technology, however, began to change the situation dramatically. As early as 1712 Thomas Newcomer first unveiled his steam-driven piston engine, which allowed the more efficient pumping of deep mines. Steam engines improved rapidly as the century advanced, and were put to greater and greater use. More efficient and powerful engines were employed in coalmines, textile mills and dozens of other heavy industries. By 1800 perhaps 2,000 steam engines were eventually at work in Britain.

New inventions in iron manufacturing, particularly those perfected by the Darby family of Shropshire, allowed for stronger and more durable metals to be produced. The use of steam engines in coalmining also ensured that a cheap and reliable supply of the iron industry's essential raw material was available: coal was now king.

Factories

The spinning of cotton into threads for weaving into cloth had traditionally taken place in the homes of textile workers. In 1769, however, Richard Arkwright patented his 'water frame', that allowed large-scale spinning to take place on just a single machine. This was followed shortly afterwards by James Hargreaves' 'spinning jenny', which further revolutionized the process of cotton spinning.

The weaving process was similarly improved by advances in technology. Edmund Cartwright's power loom, developed in the 1780s, allowed for the mass production of the cheap and light cloth that was desirable both in Britain and around the Empire. Steam technology would produce yet more change. Constant power was now available to drive the dazzling array of industrial machinery in textiles and other industries, which were installed up and down the country.

New 'manufactories' (an early word for 'factory') were the result of all these new technologies. Large industrial buildings usually employed one central source of power to drive a whole network of machines. Richard Arkwright's cotton factories in Nottingham and Cromford, for example, employed nearly 600 people by the 1770s, including many small children, whose nimble hands made light-work of spinning. Other industries flourished under the factory system. In Birmingham, James Watt and Matthew Boulton established their huge foundry and metal works in Shoo, where nearly 1,000 people were employed in the 1770s making buckles, boxes and buttons, as well as the parts for new steam engines.

Though not all factories were bad places to work, many were dismal and highly dangerous. Some factories were likened to prisons or barracks, where workers encountered harsh discipline enforced by factory owners. Many children were sent there from workhouses or orphanages to work long hours in hot, dusty conditions, and were forced to crawl through narrow spaces between fast-moving machinery. A working day of 12 hours was not uncommon, and accidents happened frequently.

Transport

The growing demand for coal after 1750 revealed serious problems with Britain's transport system. Though many mines stood close to rivers or the sea, the shipping of coal was slowed down by unpredictable tides and weather. Because of the growing demand for this essential raw material, many mine owners and industrial speculators began financing new networks of canals, in order to link their mines more effectively with the growing centers of population and industry. The early canals were small but highly beneficial. In 1761, for example, the Duke of Bridgewater opened a canal between his colliery at Wesley and the rapidly growing town of Manchester. Within weeks of the canal's opening the price of coal in Manchester halved. Other canal building schemes were quickly authorized by Acts of Parliament, in order to link up an expanding network of rivers and waterways. By 1815, over 2,000 miles of canals were in use in Britain, carrying thousands of tons of raw materials and manufactured goods by horse-drawn barge.

Most roads were in a terrible state early in this period. Many were poorly maintained and even major routes flooded during the winter. Journeys by stagecoach were long and uncomfortable. London in particular suffered badly when wagons and carts were bogged down in poor conditions and were left unable to deliver food to markets. Faced with these difficulties, local authorities applied for 'Turnpike Acts' that allowed for new roads to be constructed, paid for out of tolls placed on passing traffic. New techniques in road construction, developed by pioneering engineers such as John McAdam and Thomas Telford, led to the great 'road boom' of the 1780s.

The improvements achieved by 18th century road builders were breathtaking. By the 1830s the stagecoach journey from London to Edinburgh took just two days, compared to nearly two weeks only half a century before.

The Workers Movement from 1848 to 1917-From Independence to Power

For the first time in history the working class had shown itself as an independent force in society. It had in the revolutionary turmoil, imposed its own demands on the government. It fought a four day battle on the barricades in defense of its interests. Independent in the sense that they did not follow the political leadership of the liberal bourgeoisie that is the political leadership of the private owners of the means of production, the capitalists.

With the failure of either of the major contending classes to gain secure control of society, the capitalists turned to the rule of the army. The army took power into its own hands but guaranteed peaceful and profitable conditions for capitalist expansion. This situation is known as Bonaparte's after Napoleon Bonaparte who performed the same role for the bourgeoisie in 1799. The workers had been easily defeated as they had put their faith in a government talking shop called the Luxembourg Commission. While workers talked with the boss's representatives the capitalists were preparing to physically crush the workers' movement. Following the defeat of the revolutions of 1848 a period of reaction followed. Industry grew quickly and production dramatically increased. In the process small peasants went to the wall and small business (the petty bourgeoisie) was hit badly, but the size of the working class increased.

England becomes the workshop of the world. France was developing, but small scale development still dominated.

In this situation the labour movement made little progress. Wages were high, and there was little unemployment. The unions were organized along narrow craft lines. They were conservative and fearful of political action, and they were prepared to support the liberal bourgeoisie. In 1859 a crisis broke out and the capitalists sought to put the burden of the crisis on to the backs of the workers. There were many strikes particularly in the building trades in 1859/60. These forced the unions to organize on a larger scale and in 1861 the first London Trades Council was formed. (Chris Gaffney)

In France

The defeats of 1848 and the large number of petty bourgeois led to the dominance of the ideas of Proudhon. Proudhon opposed socialism; rather he argued that the workers should fight to establish credit unions and co-ops within capitalism.

He opposed political struggle and strikes, and urged passivity towards the state. His goal was a society of small producers. He advocated private property but was opposed to large scale capitalism.

The ideas of Proudhon fitted the small scale producers who dominated French production.

The other tendency in the French labour movement was the Blanquettes, who paid no attention to social and political questions. They were a conspiratorial group who looked for a chance to stage a coup d'état to transform society.

In Germany

The growth of capitalism brought into existence a labour movement. In 1863 Lassalle urged a break with the liberal bourgeoisie and established the Union of German Workers. Lassalle opposed class struggle, preferring negotiations with the bosses. He saw the ballot box as the way to improve the lot of the workers.

In 1869 the German Social Democratic Worker's Party was established.

The First International

Labour activities increased throughout Europe in the 1860's. The American civil war (1861-1865) starved Europe of cotton and textile workers in particular were hit. The British and French workers' organizations exchanged greetings of solidarity and co-operated in joint activity. This was the first step in the establishment of the First International. This co-operation was extended in 1863 when the workers of a number of European countries supported the Polish people in their revolt against Russian rule. Further co-operation against scabs led to the establishment of the International Working Men's Association in 1863. Karl Marx was elected onto its committee and wrote its first manifesto.

From the first the International was never of one view. It contained in it the major ideological tendencies operating in the labour movements of Europe. The Congresses held in 1867 and 1868 saw the struggle between the ideas of Proudhon and Marx. The International's help to the French strikes in 1869 led to a ban on the International in France but it also led to a decline of Proudhon's influence. The International in its resolutions established the idea that the workers would need to win power to win their liberation. After Proudhon a bigger challenge rose in the form of the anarchist Bakunin. He believed:

- That we should forget day to day struggles and prepare for insurrection.
- In the political and economic equality of the classes and was against class struggle.
- That Marx exaggerated the importance of the working class and that the revolution would be led by those who suffered most like the unemployed, women, and various minority groups.

The anarchists were stronger in Italy, Spain and Switzerland than elsewhere. They dissolved their Anarchist alliance and joined the International. The differences between them and Marx would come to a head during the period of the Paris Commune.

The Paris Commune 1871

In 1870 war broke out between Prussia (the most powerful kingdom of Germany) and the French. The French Emperor Louis Napoleon, the nephew of Napoleon Bonaparte, was, unlike Bonaparte, a rotten general and soon Prussian forces were threatening Paris.

Louis Napoleon fled but the ruling class Government of National Defense that took his place soon showed itself to be a 'Government of National Betrayal' to use Marx's expression. They were far more concerned with defeating their own working class than they were in defending France. On January 28th 1871 they concluded an armistice with the Prussian Bismarck, but were hampered in their efforts by the existence of the National Guard. The National Guard based in Paris was overwhelmingly working class. It was armed and ready to defend Paris. When the Government attempted to steal the cannon of the National Guard they were spotted by women early in the morning. There was an uprising and the National Guard took control of Paris. With no one group dominating and no clear leadership the National Guard became fearful of the responsibility of power and handed power over to an elected Commune.

Marx believed that the government of the Commune was the working class in power and that this was the form in which the emancipation of the working class would happen. It also showed Marx that the working class could not simply lay hold of the existing state apparatus and wield it for its own purposes. Rather that it would have to demolish the existing state and replaced it with a state of its own.

The Growth of Reformism

After the Commune there was a flourishing period for capitalism encouraged by the expansion to the non- capitalist world particularly in the 1870's and 1880's. The growth of huge industrial combines and bank concentrations ushered in the era of imperialism.

The Marxists saw the rivalry by the great powers for markets as eventually leading to a worldwide war, but the atmosphere was ripe for a belief in reforms because

- There had been no crisis or war in Europe for 20 years.
- The workers had won reforms as capitalism was prepared to concede reforms to the workers rather than risk industrial unrest which might interrupt production.
- Capitalist economic crisis developed from contradictions between capitalism's permanent tendency to extend production and the limited capacity of the capitalist market to consume it.

Credit had the effect of ever extending the productive capacity beyond the capacity of society to consume it. At the moment of crisis when credit could have saved the day for capital, it takes flight and is quite useless. It calls in its debts and so intensifies the crisis.

Credit also assists the concentration of capital and weakens the vitality of smaller undertakings which collapse at the first sign of the crisis. As for cartels they could solve the crisis only if they were universal, but in fact they were essentially national, and in competition with each other. Lastly Rosa showed that the unions could not end capitalism. They were defensive organizations of the workers which helped the workers get the market value of their labour power in the capitalist market. They were not the instruments of the destruction of that law which treats human labour power as a commodity.

Rosa showed that Marx's theory of the crisis of overproduction really only applies when the world market was fully developed and could no longer be endlessly enlarged. Thus the crises prior to 1873 were crises of sudden growth as the world market was still expanding. Credit and the growth of cartels would not save this situation but rather it would hasten this development of the world market and so bring on the capitalist crisis that much sooner.

The Russian Revolution

Marx had supposed that a socialist revolution would occur as a result of the overspending of conditions in advanced capitalism. Russia was only beginning to enter a capitalist phase, and in the country at least, little had changed since the 17th century. Serfdom had only been formally abolished in 1863 but even this changed little for the peasants who were 75% of the population. 90% of the people were illiterate and some 30.000 landowners owned as much as land as 30 million peasants.

From 1870 on industrialization began, sponsored by the czarist state. This was largely non - indigenous capital and was drawn mainly from the British and French. Unlike Britain for example, the development of industry did not go through a long period of development from small to large industry but started at the most advanced level. Consequently within the predominately feudal landscape we find isolated concentrations of the most advanced industry employing thousands of workers. These workers had no rights, no legal unions and no parliamentary tradition to incline them to adjust to their wretched conditions. From the first the option of reform did not exist for these workers.

In France in 1789 it was the bourgeoisie that had led the peasants against feudalism and many of the Russian Marxists expected that this would happen in a similar way in Russia. In Russia the native bourgeoisie was small, a Johnny come lately, and dominated by foreign capital. It was also dependent on the Czar and the state. The working class, though it was only 25% of the population, was concentrated and had a social strength out of all proportion to its numbers. As Trotsky had argued and after April 1917 Lenin had agreed, it was the working class and not the bourgeoisie that would have to lead the peasants in revolution against the Czarist state.

Literature of a Revolutionary Period

Before a great revolution, nearly all literature expresses dissatisfaction and distress over social conditions, voicing suffering and indignation. There are many works of this kind in the world. But these expressions of suffering and indignation have no influence on the revolution, for mere complaints are powerless. Those who oppress you will ignore them. The mouse may squeak and even produce fine literature, yet the cat will gobble it up without any consideration. So a nation with only a literature of complaint is hopeless, because it stops short at that. Just as in a lawsuit, when the defeated party starts distributing accounts of his grievances his opponent knows that he cannot afford to go on and the case is as good as wound up, so the literature of complaints, like proclaiming one's grievances, gives the oppressors a sense of security. Some nations stop complaining when it proves useless and become silent nations, growing more and more decadent. Witness Egypt, Arabia, Persia and India all of which have no voice. But nations with inner strength which dare rebel when complaints prove useless wake up to the facts and their lamentations change into roars of anger. When such literature appears it heralds revolt, and because people are enraged the works written just before the outbreak of revolution often voice their fury their determination to resist, taking vengeance. Literature of this kind heralded the October Revolution. But, there are exceptions too, as in the case of Poland where although there had long been the literature of vengeance-the country owed its recovery to the Great War in Europe.

During a great revolution, literature disappears and there is silence for, swept up in the tide of revolution, all turn from shouting to action and are so busy making revolution that there is no time to talk of literature. Again, that is a period of poverty when men are so hard put to it to find bread that they are in no mood to talk of literature. **Conservatives**, staggered by the high tide of revolution, are too enraged and stunned to sing what passes with them for "literature".

When the revolution has triumphed, there is less social tension and men are better off, then literature is written again. There are two types of literature in this period. One extols the revolution and sings its praise, because progressive writers are impressed by the changes and advances in society, the destruction of the old and the construction of the new. Rejoicing in the downfall of old institutions, they sing the praises of the new construction. The second type of writing to appear after a revolution referred dirge the destruction of the old. Some consider this "counter-revolutionary literature",

Though a revolution has taken place, there are many of the old schools in society who cannot change overnight into new people. Since their minds are full of old ideas, when their surroundings gradually change, affecting their whole mode of life, they think back to the good old days and hanker after the old society. Because they keep harking back, they express most old-fashioned, outmoded sentiments, and create this literature. All works of this kind are mournful, expressing the writers' discomfort. The evident success of the new construction and the ruin of the old institutions make them chant dirges. But this longing for the past and this chanting of dirges means that the revolution has been carried out. Without a revolution, the old people would still be in power and would not chant dirges.

Only China today has neither type of literature either dirges for the old or praise for the new for the Chinese revolution is not yet accomplished. This is still the transitional period, a busy time for revolutionaries. There is still a good deal of the old literature left, though, practically everything in the papers being written in the old style. This means that the Chinese revolution has brought about very few changes in our society, scarcely affecting the conservatives at all, and therefore the old school can still hold aloof. The fact that all or nearly all the writing in the Canton papers is old proves that society here is equally untouched by the revolution; hence there are no paeans for the new, no dirges for the old, and the province of Kwangtung remains as it was ten years ago. Not only so, there are no complaints or protests either. We see trade unions taking part in demonstrations, but with government sanction not revolting against oppression. This is merely revolution by government order. Because China has not changed, we have no songs of mournful yearning for the past and no new marching songs. In Soviet Russia, however, they have both types. Their old writers who have fled abroad write mostly dirges for the dead, while their new literature strives to make headway. Though no great works have yet appeared, there is already a good deal of new writing and they have passed from the period of raging to that of paeans.

Some writers today use the common people , workers and peasants as material for their novels and poems, and this has also been called people's literature when actually it is nothing of the sort, for the people have not yet opened theft mouths. These works voice the sentiments of onlookers, who put words in the people's mouths. Though some of our present men of letters are poor, they are all better off than workers and peasants, otherwise they would not have had the money to study and would not be able to write. Their works may seem to come from the people, but in fact they do not. They are not real stories of the people. Now some writers have started recording folk-songs in the belief that here we have the authentic voice of the people, for these are sung by the common folk.(Narodniks)

The majority of Americans in the Revolutionary period were laboring people of one sort or another. In the countryside, their perspectives and activities became largely indistinguishable from that of the general population. However, their numbers in the cities and towns were large enough to define a distinctive approach to the problems of the Revolution. The populations of only twenty communities had grown beyond 3,000, but Philadelphia, New York, and Boston had many times that number. A large proportion of these depended on the earnings of unskilled day labor or skilled craftsmanship. Among the latter, one advanced through the rank of apprentice to journeyman to master. Broadly described as "mechanics," these urban artisans had disproportionate importance because of their location in the seaport cities. There, several of the more well-off and influential craftsmen like Paul Revere sat in the inner circles of Boston's Loyal Nine, the secret steering body of the opposition. Revere, like Benjamin Franklin was no mere manual laborer but a prosperous businessman who employed other artisans.

Nevertheless, the radical strategy of blocking enforcement of imperial measures required mobilizing craftsmen and laborers who had hitherto played only a marginal role in colonial political life. These urban commoners made their views felt by following street leaders like Ebenezer Macintosh, the Boston shoemaker in thwarting the Stamp Act of 1765. After initially leading this "mob" on a rampage against the symbols and property of the authorities, such men proved to be reliable, plebeian allies of the rebellious local elites.

After the 1766 repeal of the Stamp Act, the British imposed a series of duties on goods imported into the colonies. Unwilling to risk mobilizing "mobs" they could not control, opposition leaders turned to no importation. This new strategy had a particular appeal to the mechanics as domestic manufacturers of goods. While artisans tended more readily to favor the boycott of British imports, some colonial merchants immersed in Transatlantic trade, politics and culture lost whatever enthusiasm they had for this particular approach.

As a result, artisans began playing a more independent role in the resistance strategy. More or less distinct committees, associations and societies of mechanics began to appear under the general auspices of radical leaders. Craftsmen clashed with the authorities in such incidents as New York's Battle of Golden Hill and the Boston Massacre. As the British imposed the Tea Tax, craftsmen, laborers and seamen provided the self-invited participants in the "Tea Party."As the actual fighting began, craftsmen and laborers provided disproportionate numbers to the militias and Continental army units.

While British occupation scattered the patriot peoples of Boston and New York, craftsmen at Philadelphia followed the local radical leaders in overthrowing the old Pennsylvania proprietary government. These also provided the political weight to secure the most democratic state constitution of the Revolutionary period. In most of the urban centers, women of the laboring classes provided the front line proponents of rigorous and militant actions to curb profiteering and regulate the prices of foodstuffs and other "necessaries" of life. Within the army, such grievances contributed to the eruption of the 1781 "mutiny" in which Philadelphia workingmen in the Pennsylvania Line waged what its historian called a "well-managed strike."

In the end, the victory for American Independence only partially realized the aspirations of such laboring people. Despite the success for which both Revere and Macintosh had worked, the former ended his days as a wealthy and respected Boston manufacturer basking in the fame of his 1775 ride, while Macintosh died forgotten in a Vermont poorhouse. For the Revolutionary generation, latter was much more characteristic of the fate of workingmen-participants and their families.

Nevertheless, independence had dissolved the social contract, leaving much open for renegotiation. Men with close personal ties to the development of the mechanic resistance and to the Revolution went on to organize other workers within their crafts and wage strikes for better wages and conditions. Samuel Lecount, a Philadelphia printers and Continental veteran shared both a record of his commitment to liberty and participation in the 1786 strike. Such forgotten men and their children established the first labor movement in American history.

Over time, the increasing proportions of property less workers, began rewriting the Declaration of Independence to reflect their grievances. In doing so, they discussed a social contract of the workplace, asserted a liberty that embraced a living wage and decent standard of living, and warned that violations of this understanding would lead to independent actions by workers. In this spirit, their organizations continued to celebrate the Fourth of July and cherish all such associations with the Revolutionary generation.

At the close of the war, Dr. Benjamin Rush wisely advised against confusing American Independence with "the American Revolution." The latter he wrote, had just begun. The struggles of the laboring people of the Revolutionary generation demonstrates that the "American Revolution" is still being fought(Mark A.Lause)

Marxian Ideology

Engels and Marx founded the social and economic system of marxism in the 19th century. Essentially, it is the opposite of capitalism.Capitalism is based on private ownership and motivation by profit. Marx criticizes capitalism for its tendency to abouse the working man, or "the proletariat"by paing a wage that barely guarentees the workers survival.

Instead, marxism utilizes socialisms concept of public ownership.

Marxism theorizes that in order to remove the proletariat from its poor economic situation, a socialist revolution must occur to remove the unconcerned ruling class from government. Following the revoluon, a nrw, socialist government is created that subsequently becomes communist in nature.Marxist criticism is the belief that literature reflects this class struggle and materialism. It looks at how literature functions in relation to other aspects of the superstructure, particularly other articulations of ideology. Like, feminist critics, it investigates how literature can work as a force for social change, or as a reaffirmation of existing conditions.Like new historicism, it examines how history influences literature; the difference is that marxism focuses on the lower classes.

General Principles of Marxist Criticism

It promotes the idea that literature should be a tool in the revolutionary struggle.Besides It's attempts to clarify the relationship of literary work to social reality and political in nature.It aims to at an interpretation of literary text in order to define the political dimensions of literary work.It belives that the literary work has always a relationship to the society.However, It judges literature by how it represents the main struggles for power going on that time, how it may influence those struggles.

Materialism Vs Spirituality

Marx averred that reality is material not spiritual. We are not spiritual beings but socially constructed ones.As, critics, we are tasked to examine the relationship among socio economic groups in order to achieve insight into ourselves and our society.

Art Literature and Ideologies

The dominant class or higher class do control art, literature, and and ideologies. Marxist critics should identify the ideology of the work and point out its worth and deficiencies and apporach the text with an eye for how the characters interact. Marxist thought relies on relationships between individuals, and even those aspects of relationships that are social can be part of a marxist critique.Evaluate the vocational roles of all characters. The marxist critique includes a focus on a "class system" where the vocations of characters provide the most direct reference to their place within this system. Look at the level of luxury that each individual has and how much they have to work.

Assess the Role of Government in the Piece of Literature

Is it draconian? Laisssez –faire? Marxist thought relies on government as a model for iberty and also for communalism : look at the tools that government uses. Does the government, inoliciting citizenship, appeal to the apitalist endencies of individuals ? It has used marxist writers as a guide. Pick ideas outlined by Marxist writers of past eras and apply them to your particular study. As a general guideline, ."rules" shouldn't be over emphasized in literary criticism. It does not have to be technical,just go from a general "Marxist viewpoint and tell something about the story.

Marx's Critique of Capitalism

First, Marx does not offer a theory of price (as is the case with mainstream neoclassical theory (micro-economics). Instead, his interest is in seeing what the mechanisms of capitalist reproduction are. That is, what are the processes of capitalist production, what must happen, what agents must believe, what are the problems that need to be solved if the system is to keep going *Capital* is subtitled, "A critique of Political Economy" in just this sense. Second, Marx would not deny that there are huge differences between concrete capitalistic *societies,* e.g., the capitalism which he studied, American capitalism in the 1990s, Japanese or Philippine capitalism. He proceeded by *abstraction* and found what he thought were the essential or defining features of any capitalist society however capitalist societies are, e.g., in their actual class arrangements, culture or politics. There was, for him, an ideal configuration. E.g., liberalism and capitalism work well together (for reasons which are not hard to find); but no society has to fit exactly this ideal configuration of elements.

Commodity Production

While all societies produce what they need (and usually also a social surplus), the form which products take when production is organized for generalized exchange is the commodity, goods and services which are sold. If there is to be exchange, products must have a use value in the plain sense that they are wanted for the properties they have. But their exchange ratios (why something costs twice as much as something else) cannot be explained in terms of the properties which give them use-value. The fundamental insight of the so-called "labor theory of value" is that commodities share in but one thing: they are all products of human labor. But not only are there all sorts of commodities, but there are all sorts of labor. How can products produced by different kinds of labor be commensurate? (On what dimension can they be compared and put into ratios?) Marx answers that when we exchange, we reduce 'heterogeneous" labor to "abstract" labor. As he writes: "whenever, by an exchange, we equate as values our different products, by that very act, we also equate, as human labor, the different kinds of labor expended upon them" What is produced may or may not represent what Marx calls "socially necessary labor-time," roughly, the optimal use and allocation of labor, given existing technical conditions. (The tendency of markets to move in this direction is what Marx calls "the law of value." It compares to Smith's "natural price." For Marx, "value" (exchange value) equals price if and only if socially necessary labor-time was employed in production.)

The "money-form" conceals both the "absurdity" of the reduction of heterogeneous labor to abstract labor-time and the fact that this allocation may or may not be "rational" (in the appropriate sense). This is the point of the comparison to Robinson Crusoe and to a community of people rationally allocating their labor-time. Robinson knows how much time he can put into his various projects if he is to maintain himself and he decides what to do when. A "communist" community, having established its goals and resources, would do likewise. Feudalism (and similar pre-capitalist forms) provides a good intermediate case. The peasant's plant and harvest according to the seasons. Everyone is kept in his place by the ruling lord who holds power and decides what he will take from the serfs. In feudalism, Marx says, "there is no necessity for labour and its products to assume a fantastic form different from their reality Payments are in kind and "the social relations between Individuals in the performance of their labour, appear at all events as their mutual personal relations, and are not disguised under the shape of social relations between the products of labor" (Brewer-Marxist Theory)

Commodity Fetishism and Alienation

It is just this "disguises" which Marx calls "commodity fetishism," a form of Alienation in which "a definite social relation between men assumes, in their eyes, the fantastic form of a relation between things". Our labor and our products are "priced." This defines us as commodities and defines our relations to one another. "The value of a man," as Hobbes had already noted, "is his worth, or what would be given for the use of his powers." Similarly, when we look for job, we say that "the market" determines what jobs there are and what they pay. When we shop or look for housing, the "market" determines what is available and what we have to pay. We "relate" to one other impersonally as mutually interdependent commodities engaged in generalized exchange. Marx concludes that "political economy from Adam Smith to Ricardo and with antecedents in Hobbes and Locke, has indeed analyzed, however incompletely, value and its magnitude....But it has never asked the question why labour is represented by the value of its product and labour-time by the magnitude of that value. These formulae, which bear it stamped upon them in unmistakable letters that they belong to a state of society, in which the process of production has the mastery over man, instead of being controlled by him, such formulae appear... to be as much a self-evident necessity imposed by Nature as productive labour itself" (Hobson)

Surplus Value

In nearly all known societies there is a social surplus. **Surplus labor** is the labor time not used to maintain the worker. What counts as "maintenance" is conventional and varies historically. Thus, it may include not merely a dwelling, but a dwelling of certain sort. There must be surplus labor if cathedrals, e.g., are to be built and lords to be fed and clothed. In capitalism, however, surplus labor takes the form of **surplus value**: value created by the worker which is not necessary for his "maintenance." Surplus value is the source of capitalist profit. Consider the series C-M-C1 where C represents commodities and M represents money. In this series, if buyers and sellers are "rational," the money the seller of C got could only buy C1 if its value equaled C. unless somebody cheats (or is not "rational") no Profit is possible. Consider then M-C- M1. If M1 is greater than M, then there is only one commodity that can be purchased, labor-power, since it alone can create value. This is fairly obvious: no capitalist hires somebody to work for him unless that worker gets paid less than the value of what he produces. Of course, machines increase the efficiency of workers, but not only do machines need workers but they also represent "concealed labor power:" they were also made by humans. Parenthetically, this fact is critical for Marx's argument that there will be tendency for a falling rate of profit. Capitalists, necessarily interested in cost-reduction, will try to cheapen labor costs, either by increasing the efficiency of workers or by finding workers who will work at lower wages. But this also reduces the value of the product and hence, the source of profit. (Emmanuel)

Exploitation

In slavery and serfdom, exploitation is obvious. Everyone knows who has power and that coercion is available to enforce who gets what. In capitalism, as social relations are "disguised" and relations are literally, "impersonal," being relations between things, so is exploitation. Marx agrees with conventional economists, who insist that in capitalism, workers get "what they worth," since as before, equals exchange for equals. So workers are not cheated by employers and no coercion is used against them. They accept their wages "voluntarily" and thus think of themselves as "free." But "wage slavery" is still slavery since workers must sell their labor-power to those who own the means of life the defining feature of capitalism and the fundamental division of class in capitalism. But since only labor can create value and profit has its source in surplus value, exploitation in capitalism is systemic (structural) even while it is "disguised." (Hiller Steiner)

Capitalism, Law and Government

The foregoing all depends upon a juridical system which defines private property, contract and the rights of men. Capitalist reproduction can minimize coercion if people accept liberal ideology including, critically, a "republican" form of regime in which they are "sovereign people" even if, on the one hand, as Rousseau, had noted, they have alienated all their power to "governments" and even if, accordingly, their governments act only to reproduce capitalism. (Rawls)

Karl Marx and Frederick Engels

The industrial revolution in England & French revolution In Karl Marx and Friedrich Engels we have two individuals who have greatly influenced human thought. The personality of Engels recedes somewhat into the background as compared to Marx. We shall subsequently see their interrelation. As regards Marx one is not likely to find in the history of the nineteenth century a man who, by his activity and his scientific attainments, had as much to do as he, with determining the thought and actions of a succession of generations in a great number of countries. Marx has been dead more than forty years. Yet he is still alive. His thought continues to influence, and to give direction to, the intellectual development of the most remote countries, countries which never heard of Marx when he was alive.

We shall attempt to discern the conditions and the surroundings in which Marx and Engels grew and developed. Every one is a product of a definite social milieu. Every genius creating something new, does it on the basis of what has been accomplished before him. He does not sprout forth from a vacuum. Furthermore, to really determine the magnitude of a genius, one must first ascertain the antedating achievements, the degree of the intellectual development of society, the social forms into which this genius was born and from which he drew his psychological and physical sustenance. And so, to understand Marx -- and this is a practical application of Marx's own method - we shall first proceed to study the historical background of his period and its influence upon him.

Karl Marx was born on the 5th of May, 1818, in the city of Treves, in Rhenish Prussia; Engels, on the 28th of November, 1820, in the city of Barmen of the same province. It is significant that both were born in Germany, in the Rhine province, and at about the same time. During their impressionable and formative years of adolescence, both Marx and Engels came under the influence of the stirring events of the early thirties of the nineteenth century. The years 1830 and 1831 were revolutionary years; in 1830 the July Revolution occurred in France. It swept all over Europe from West to East. It even reached Russia and brought about the Polish Insurrection of 1831.

But the July Revolution in itself was only a culmination of another more momentous revolutionary upheaval, the consequences of which one must know to understand the historical setting in which Marx and Engels were brought up. The history of the nineteenth century, particularly that third of it which had passed before Marx and Engels had grown into socially conscious youths, was characterized by two basic facts: The Industrial Revolution in England, and the Great Revolution in France. The Industrial Revolution in England began approximately in 1760 and extended over a prolonged period. Having reached its zenith towards the end of the eighteenth century, it came to an end at about 1830. The term "Industrial Revolution" belongs to Engels. It refers to that transition period, when England, at about the second half of the eighteenth century, was becoming a capitalist country. There already existed a working class, proletarians - that is, a class of people possessing no property, no means of production, and compelled therefore to sell themselves as a commodity, as human labour power, in order to gain the means of subsistence. However, in the middle of the eighteenth century, English capitalism was characterized in its methods of production by the handicraft system. It was not the old craft production where each petty enterprise had its master, its two or three journeymen, and a few apprentices. This traditional handicraft was being crowded out by capitalist methods of production. About the second half of the eighteenth century, capitalist production in England had already evolved into the manufacturing stage. The distinguishing feature of this manufacturing stage was an industrial method which did not go beyond the boundaries of handicraft production, in spite of the exploitation of the workers by the capitalists and the considerable size of the workrooms. From the point of view of technique and labour organization it differed from the old handicraft methods in a few respects. The capitalist brought together from a hundred to three hundred craftsmen in one large building, as against the five or six people in the small workroom heretofore. No matter what craft, given a number of workers, there soon appeared a high degree of division of labour with all its consequences. There was then a capitalist enterprise, without machines, without automatic mechanisms, but in which division of labour and the breaking up of the very method of production into a variety of partial operations had gone a long way forward. Thus it was just in the middle of the eighteenth century that the manufacturing stage reached it apogee.

Only since the second half of the eighteenth century, approximately since the sixties, have the technical bases of production themselves begun to change. Instead of the old implements, machines were introduced. This invention of machinery was started in that branch of industry which was the most important in England, in the domain of textiles. A series of inventions, one after another, radically changed the technique of the weaving and spinning trades. We shall not enumerate all the inventions. Suffice it to say that in about the eighties, both spinning and weaving looms were invented. In 1785, Watt's perfected steam-engine was invented. It enabled the manufactories to be established in cities instead of being restricted to the banks of rivers to obtain water power. This in its turn created favorable conditions for the centralization and concentration of production. After the introduction of the steam-engine, attempts to utilize steam as motive power were being made in many branches of industry. But progress was not as rapid as is sometimes claimed in books. The period from 1760 to 1830 is designated as the period of the great Industrial Revolution.

Imagine a country where for a period of seventy years new inventions were incessantly introduced, where production was becoming ever more concentrated, where a continuous process of expropriation, ruin and annihilation of petty handicraft production, and the destruction of small weaving and spinning workshops were inexorably going on. Instead of craftsmen there came an ever-increasing host of proletarians. Thus in place of the old class of workers, which had begun to develop in the sixteenth and seventeenth centuries, and which in the first half of the eighteenth century still constituted a negligible portion of the population of England, there appeared towards the end of the eighteenth and the beginning of the nineteenth centuries, a class of workers which comprised a considerable portion of the population, and which determined and left a definite imprint on all contemporary social relations. Together with this Industrial Revolution there occurred a certain concentration in the ranks of the working class itself. This fundamental change in economic relations, this uprooting of the old weavers and spinners from their habitual modes of life, was superseded by conditions which forcefully brought to the mind of the worker the painful difference between yesterday and today. yesterday there were inherited firmly established relations between the employers and the workers. Now everything was changed and the employers relentlessly threw out of employment tens and hundreds of these workers. In response to this basic change in the conditions of their very existence the workers reacted energetically. Endeavoring to get rid of these new conditions they rebelled. It is obvious that their unmitigated hatred, their burning indignation should at first have been directed against the visible symbol of this new and powerful revolution, the machine, which to them personified all the misfortune, all the evils of the new system. No wonder that at the beginning of the nineteenth century a series of revolts of the workers directed against the machine and the new technical methods of production took place. These revolts attained formidable proportions in England in 1815. (The weaving loom was finally perfected in 1813). About that time the movement spread to all industrial centers. From a purely elemental force, it was soon transformed into an organized resistance with appropriate slogans and efficient leaders. This movement directed against the introduction of machinery is known in history as the movement of the Luddites.

According to one version this name was derived from the name of a worker; according to another, it is connected with a mythical general, Lud, whose name the workers used in signing their proclamations. The ruling classes, the dominant oligarchy, directed the most cruel repressions against the Luddites. For the destruction of a machine as well as for an attempt to injure a machine, a death penalty was imposed. Many a worker was sent to the gallows. There was a need for a higher degree of development of this workers' movement and for more adequate revolutionary propaganda. The workers had to be informed that the fault was not with the machines, but with the conditions under which these machines were being used. A movement which was aiming to mould the workers into a class-conscious revolutionary mass, able to cope with definite social and political problems was just then beginning to show vigorous signs of life in England. Leaving out details, we must note, however, that this movement of 1815-1817 had its beginnings at the end of the eighteenth century. To understand, however, the significance of it, we must turn to France; for without a thorough grasp of the influence of the French Revolution, it will be difficult to understand the beginnings of the English labour movement. The French Revolution began in 1789, and reached its climax in 1793. From 1794, it began to diminish in force. This brought about, within a few years, the establishment of Napoleon's military dictatorship. In 1799, Napoleon accomplished his coup d'état. After having been a Consul for five years, he proclaimed himself Emperor and ruled over France up to 1815. (David Riazanov's)

At the end of the eighteenth century, France was a country ruled by an absolute monarchy, not unlike that of Tsarist Russia. But the power was actually in the hands of the nobility and the clergy, who, for monetary compensation of one kind or another, sold a part of their influence to the growing financial-commercial bourgeoisie. Under the influence of a strong revolutionary movement among the masses of the people - the petty producers, the peasants, the small and medium tradesmen who had no privileges - the French monarch was compelled to grant some concessions. He convoked the so-called Estates General. In the struggle between two distinct social groups - the city poor and the privileged classes - power fell into the hands of the revolutionary petty bourgeoisie and the Paris workers. This was on August 10, 1792. This domination expressed itself in the rule of the Jacobins headed by Robespierre and Marat, and one may also add the name of Danton. For two years France was in the hands of the insurgent people. In the vanguard stood revolutionary Paris. The Jacobins, as representatives of the petty bourgeoisie, pressed the demands of their class to their logical conclusions. The leaders, Marat, Robespierre and Danton, were petty-bourgeois democrats who had taken upon themselves the solution of the problem which confronted the entire bourgeoisie, that is, the purging of France of all the remnants of the feudal regime, the creating of free political conditions under which private property would continue unhampered and under which small proprietors would not be hindered from receiving reasonable incomes through honest exploitation of others. In this strife for the creation of new political conditions and the struggle against feudalism, in this conflict with the aristocracy and with a united Eastern Europe which was attacking France, the Jacobins, Robespierre and Marat have performed the part of revolutionary leaders. In their fight against all of Europe they had to resort to revolutionary propaganda. To hurl the strength of the populace, the mass, against the strength of the feudal lords and the kings, they brought into play the slogan: "War to the palace, peace to the cottage." On their banners they inscribed the slogan: "Liberty, Equality, and Fraternity."

These first conquests of the French Revolution were reflected in the Rhine province. There, too, Jacobin societies were formed. Many Germans went as volunteers into the French army. In Paris some of them took part in all the revolutionary associations. During all this time the Rhine province was greatly influenced by the French Revolution, and at the beginning of the nineteenth century, the younger generation was still brought up under the potent influence of the heroic traditions of the Revolution. Even Napoleon, who was a usurper, was obliged, in his war against the old monarchical and feudal Europe, to lean upon the basic victories of the French Revolution, for the very reason that he was a usurper, the foe of the feudal regime. He commenced his military career in the revolutionary army. The vast mass of the French soldiers, ragged and poorly armed, fought the superior Prussian forces, and defeated them. They won by their enthusiasm, their numbers. They won because before shooting bullets they hurled manifestoes, thus demoralizing and disintegrating the enemy's armies. Nor did Napoleon in his campaigns shun revolutionary propaganda. He knew quite well that cannon was a splendid means, but he never, to the last days of his life, disdained the weapon of revolutionary propaganda - the weapon that disintegrates so efficiently the armies of the adversary.

The influence of the French Revolution spread further East; it even reached St. Petersburg. At the news of the fall of the Bastille, people embraced and kissed one another even there.

There was already in Russia a small group of people who reacted quite intelligently to the events of the French Revolution, the outstanding figure being Radishchev. This influence was more or less felt in all European countries; even in that very England which stood at the head of nearly all the coalition armies directed against France. It was strongly felt not only by the petty-bourgeois elements but also by the then numerous laboring population which came into being as a result of the Industrial Revolution. In the years 1791 and 1792 the Corresponding

Society, the first English revolutionary labour organization, made its appearance. It assumed such an innocuous name merely to circumvent the English laws which prohibited any society from entering into organizational connections with societies in other towns. By the end of the eighteenth century, England had a constitutional government. She already had known two revolutions - one in the middle, the other at the end, of the seventeenth century. *[1642 and 1688]* She was regarded as the freest country in the world. Although clubs and societies were allowed, not one of them was permitted to unite with the other. To overcome this interdict those societies, which were made up of workers, hit upon the following method: They formed Corresponding Societies wherever it was possible associations which kept up a constant correspondence among themselves. At the head of the London society was the shoemaker, Thomas Hardy (1752-1832). He was a Scotchman of French extraction. Hardy was indeed what his name implied. As organizer of this society he attracted a multitude of workers, and arranged gatherings and meetings. Owing to the corrosive effect of the Industrial Revolution on the old manufactory production, the great majority of those who joined the societies were artisans shoemakers and tailors. The tailor, Francis Place, should also be mentioned in this connection, for he was a part of the subsequent history of the labour movement in England. One could mention a number of others, the majority of whom were handicraftsmen. But the name of Thomas Holcroft (1745-1809), shoemaker, poet, publicist and orator, who played an important role at the end of the eighteenth century, must be given.

In 1792, when France was declared a republic, this Corresponding Society availed itself of the aid of the French ambassador in London and secretly dispatched an address, in which it expressed its sympathy with the revolutionary convention. This address, one of the first manifestations of international solidarity and sympathy, made a profound impression upon the convention. It was a message from the masses of England where the ruling classes had nothing but hatred for France. The convention responded with a special resolution, and these relations between the workers' Corresponding Societies and the French Jacobins were a pretext for the English oligarchy to launch persecutions against these societies. A series of prosecutions were instituted against Hardy and others.

The fear of losing its domination impelled the English oligarchy to resort to drastic measures against the rising labour movement. Associations and societies which heretofore had been a thoroughly legal method of organization for the well-to-do bourgeois elements, and which the handicraftsmen could not by law be prevented from forming, were, in 1800, completely prohibited. The various workers' societies which had been keeping in touch with each other were particularly persecuted. In 1799 the law specifically forbade all organizations of workers in England. From 1799 to 1824 the English working class was altogether deprived of the right of free assembly and association.

The Luddite movement, whose sole purpose was the destruction of the machine, was succeeded by a more conscious struggle. The new revolutionary organizations were motivated by the determination to change the political conditions under which the workers were forced to exist. Their first demands included freedom of assembly, freedom of association, and freedom of the press. The year 1817 was ushered in with a stubborn conflict which culminated in the infamous "Manchester Massacre" of 1819. The massacre took place on St. Peter's Field, and the English workers christened it the Battle of Petrol. Enormous masses of cavalry were moved against the workers, and the skirmish ended in the death of several scores of people. Furthermore, new repressive measures, the so-called Six Acts ("Gag Laws/index.htm"), were directed against the workers. As a result of these persecutions, revolutionary strife became more intense. In 1824, with the participation of Francis Place (1771-1854), who had left his revolutionary comrades and succeeded in becoming a prosperous manufacturer, but who maintained his relations with the radicals in the House of Commons, the English workers won the famous Coalition Laws (1824-25) as a concession to the revolutionary movement. The movement in favour of creating organizations and unions through which the workers might defend themselves against the oppression of the employers, and obtain better conditions for themselves, higher wages, etc., became lawful. This marks the beginning of the English trade union movement. It also gave birth to political societies which began the struggle for universal suffrage.

Meanwhile, in France, in 1815, Napoleon had suffered a crushing defeat, and the Bourbon monarchy of Louis XVIII was established. The era of Restoration, beginning at that time, lasted approximately fifteen years. Having attained the throne through the aid of foreign intervention (Alexander I of Russia), Louis made a number of concessions to the landlords who had suffered by the Revolution. The land could not be restored to them, it remained with the peasants, but they were consoled by a compensation of a billion francs. The royal power used all its strength in an Endeavour to arrest the development of new social and political relations. It tried to rescind as many of the concessions to the bourgeoisie as it was forced to make. Owing to this conflict between the liberals and the conservatives, the Bourbon dynasty was forced to face a new revolution which broke out in July, 1830.

England which had towards the end of the eighteenth century reacted to the French Revolution by stimulating the labour movement experienced a new upheaval as a result of the July Revolution in France. There began an energetic movement for a wider suffrage. According to the English laws, that right had been enjoyed by an insignificant portion of the population, chiefly the big land owners, who not infrequently had in their dominions depopulated boroughs with only two or three electors and who, sent representatives to Parliament.

The dominant parties, actually two factions of the landed aristocracy, the Tories and the Whigs, were compelled to submit. The more liberal Whig Party, which felt the need for compromise and electoral reforms, finally won over the conservative Tories. The industrial bourgeoisie were granted the right to vote, but the workers were left in the lurch. As answer to this treachery of the liberal bourgeoisie (the ex-member of the Corresponding Society, Place, was a party to this treachery), there was formed in 1836, after a number of unsuccessful attempts, the London Workingmen's Association. This Society had a number of capable leaders. The most prominent among them were William Lovett (1800-1877) and Henry Hetherington (1792-1849). In 1837, Lovett and his comrades formulated the fundamental political demands of the working class. They aspired to organize the workers into a separate political party. They had in mind, however, not a definite working-class party which would press its special programmed as against the program of all the other parties, but one that would exercise as much influence, and play as great a part in the political life of the country, as the other parties. In this bourgeois political milieu they wanted to be the party of the working class. They had no definite aims, they did not propose any special economic program directed against the entire bourgeois society. One may best understand this, if one recalls that in Australia and New Zealand there are such labour parties, which do not aim at any fundamental changes in social conditions. They are sometimes in close coalition with the bourgeois parties in order to insure for labour a certain share of influence in the government.(Frank and Wallerstein)

The Charter, in which Lovett and his associates formulated the demands of the workers, gave the name to this Chartist movement. The Chartists advanced six demands: Universal suffrage, vote by secret ballot, parliaments elected annually, payment of members of parliament, abolition of property qualifications for members of parliament, and equalization of electoral districts. This movement began in 1837, when Marx was nineteen, and Engels seventeen years old. It reached its height when Marx and Engels were mature men.

The Revolution of 1830 in France removed the Bourbons, but instead of establishing a republic which was the aim of the revolutionary organizations of that period, it resulted in a constitutional monarchy, headed by the representatives of the Orleans dynasty. At the time of the Revolution of 1789 and later, during the Restoration period, this dynasty stood in opposition to their Bourbon relatives. Louis Philippe was the typical representative of the bourgeoisie. The chief occupation of this French monarch was the saving and hoarding of money, which delighted the hearts of the shopkeepers of Paris.

The July monarchy gave freedom to the industrial, commercial, and financial bourgeoisie. It facilitated and accelerated the process of enrichment of this bourgeoisie, and directed its onslaughts against the working class which had manifested a tendency toward organization.

In the early thirties, the revolutionary societies were composed chiefly of students and intellectuals. The workers in these organizations were few and far between. Nevertheless a workers' revolt as a protest against the treachery of the bourgeoisie broke out in 1831, in Lyons, the centre of the silk industry. For a few days the city was in the hands of the workers. They did not put forward any political demands. Their banner carried the slogan: "Live by work, or die in battle." They were defeated in the end, and the usual consequences of such defeats followed. The revolt was repeated in Lyons in 1834. Its results were even more important than those of the July Revolution. The latter stimulated chiefly the so-called democratic, petty-bourgeois elements, while the Lyons revolts exhibited, for the first time, the significance of the labour element, which had raised, though so far in only one city, the banner of revolt against the entire bourgeoisie, and had pushed the problems of the working class to the fore. The principles enunciated by the Lyons proletariat were as yet not directed against the foundations of the bourgeois system, but they were demands flung against the capitalists and against exploitation.

Thus toward the middle of the thirties in both France and England there stepped forth into the arena a new revolutionary class - the proletariat. In England, attempts were being made to organize this proletariat. In France, too, subsequent to the Lyons revolt, the proletariat for the first time tried to form revolutionary organizations. The most striking representative of this movement was Auguste Blanqui (1805-1881), one of the greatest French revolutionists. He had taken part in the July Revolution, and, impressed by the Lyons revolts which had indicated that the most revolutionary element in France were the workers, Blanqui and his friends proceeded to organize revolutionary societies among the workers of Paris. Elements of other nationalities were drawn in - German, Belgians, Swiss, etc. As a result of this revolutionary activity, Blanqui and his comrades made a daring attempt to provoke a revolt. Their aim was to seize political power and to enforce a number of measures favoring the working class. This revolt in Paris (May, 1839), terminated in defeat. Blanqui was condemned to life imprisonment. The Germans who took part in these disturbances also felt the dire consequences of defeat. Karl Scrapper (1812-1870), who will be mentioned again, and his comrades were forced to flee from France a few months later. They made their way to London and continued their work there by organizing, in 1840, the Workers' Educational Society. (Kautsky)

The Social Context in 18th Century English Literature

General features of 17th century social background The situation at the beginning of the Augustan age Agriculture Nationalism Industrial Revolution The Rise of Middle Class The Downside of the Progress Everyday Life Living Conditions Population/Transportation /Methodists. 17th century was a time of constant religious and political fighting. This age stabilized the relationships between church and state, Parliament and monarchy. These regulations provided a base for future economic and colonial expansion. %80 of the population made their living off land.

Colonial expansion improved the quality of life. Pepper and other species were brought and meat was available all year any more. People's free time was influenced by the political issues. For example, in Puritan period, all public entertainment was banned and theatres were closed. In restoration period, people started having fun again and London became a theatrical centre with various kinds of sports and plays. An economic policy called Mercantilism was put into practice. The outbreak of plague and the Great Fire of 1666 decimated the population and destroyed most of the buildings.

Rationalism: There was a prevailing spirit of optimism among the upper classes. A tendency to put faith in the rational capabilities of man in keeping with the intellectual climate of enlightenment. Romanticism raised its furiously anti-classical head. Order, reason and balance ruled the day and as a consequence of this, rational discoveries occurred. John Locke and Sir Isaac Newton played an important role in bringing about a new way of considering the world which surrounds us. Rebellion, under the guise of romanticism, was lurking impatiently in the wings in the same time. The common lands were split up and fenced into large farms by wealthy farmers. These farms enabled sheep and cattle to survive in the winter. Land Enclosures became highly efficient and provided the necessary raw material for the booming clothing industry and growing industrial revolution.

London had become a modern city, the commercial and cultural centre of England, doubling its population to one million.

Adam Smith (1723-1790) Smith criticized Brittan's trade policies and argued that labour was the real source of wealth. Lands were enclosed and common land became scare, because of that so many peasants had to find other ways of living. Many went to work in cities; the others remained in country and fell into poverty. Workhouses were built all over the country in order to deal with the increasing number of poor peasants. Many people who went to cities found job, but they had to endure subhuman living and working conditions. Factories need so much workers so the women, men and children. No allowance was given for the children, they had to work the same long hours and endure the same unhealthy environment. The people in the rural often lived in two room cottages or in mud hovels. Cities were even worse than rural areas. Many families lived in overcrowded slums without any form of sanitation. Some people didn't have beds and they slept on the floor. It is estimated that only one child in four in London became an adult. Crime was another great problem of this period. Considering the small number of wealthy people and vast number of poor, the results are predictable. (*Rabocheye Dyelo*)

CHAPTER – II

LABOUR MOVEMENT IN REVOLUTIONARY PERIOD

Capitalism

The heart of Marx's life work was the analysis of the capitalist mode of production, contained in *Capital*, volumes I-III (Marx 1961, 1957, 1962, cited below by title and volume number). The centerpiece is a theory of a closed, homogeneous, capitalist economy. Labour-power has a single price, governed by the value of labour-power, and, when prices of production are introduced (in the third volume), there is a single general rate of profit which accrues to all capitals. This is an abstraction, of course, and throughout the three volumes Marx used examples to link the abstract theory to a far more complex reality. Within the theory, though, there is no space for any differences in economic conditions between different countries. Marx's conception of the capitalist mode of production is diametrically opposed to that of dependency theorists like Frank, for whom the centre–periphery relation is an essential feature of capitalism. In this section, I shall outline the basic theory very briefly, with the focus on key concepts used by later writers. This is not a text on Marxist economic theory: there is a substantial literature on the subject for those who wish to read more (e.g. Brewer 1984; Foley 1986; Howard and King 1985). Capitalism is a particular form of *commodity production,* production of goods for sale on the market. This form of economy exists where there are many independent producers who produce goods for sale rather than for their own use. Marx distinguished between the *use value* of a commodity, the use to which it can be put, and its *exchange value,* what can be got in exchange for it. The production of use values is absolutely essential to the survival of any society, but in a commodity-producing system this is obscured by the fact that the producer is interested only in the exchange value of the product. Marx argued that exchange values are explained and determined by *(labour) values*, where the value of a commodity is defined as the *socially ecessary labour time* (measured in hours), directly or indirectly required to reproduce it. The labour theory of value has been the subject of much debate (e.g. Morishima 1973, 1974, 1976; Steedman 1975, 1977; Himmelweit and Mohun 1978; Wright 1979).The difficulty in using labour values is that goods do not, in fact, exchange at their values in a developed capitalist economy; they exchange at market prices which luctuate around prices of production (see below). In cases of joint production and in any but the simplest cases involving fixed capital, values are hard to define satisfactorily, and are liable to come out negative, or to fail to add up correctly (Steedman 1975, 1976, 1977). Very few theories of imperialism depend heavily on the labour theory of value, so labour values can be treated simply as a convenient way to set out Marx's theory. The main propositions could be restated in terms of other theories of price, but I shall use labour values, since that was how Marx did it. The heart of Marx's theory, his account of the social relations of capitalism, does not depend on the labour theory of value. Marx then asked: what is the source of the *surplus value* (roughly, profit) which accrues to a capitalist? He found the answer in the specific social relation which links a wage worker with a capitalist employer. The worker, he said, sells his *labour-power,* his capacity to work, rather than his labour. The distinction between labour power and about is crucial to the labour theory of value (the labour value of labour would be a nonsense), but it also reflects a central feature of capitalism; the actual work process, the conversion of labour-power into actual work itself, is carried out under the authority of the new owner of labour-power, its buyer, the capitalist. (Andrew Ure) The capitalist also buys *means of production* (materials, equipment, etc.) for the worker to work with. The value created by labour corresponds to the number of hours worked in (say) a day (given average conditions of production), but the wage paid by the capitalist corresponds to the *value of labour power,* that is, the labour required to reproduce a day's labour power, which is, in turn, the value of the commodities needed for the subsistence of the worker (and his family, since the worker must be Reproduced). If the value created in a day exceeds the value of a day's labour-power then there is surplus value which the capitalist can pocket when he sells the product. In terms of the relationship between the workers as a whole and capital as a whole this amounts to saying that profit (or surplus value) exists hen the workers produce more than they get. Surplus value, in other words, corresponds to a *surplus product.* For an individual capitalist, however, profit (or surplus value) depends on prices (or values), since the commodities individual workers get are not the same as those they produce; where the goods produced and consumed are not the same we cannot subtract the one from the other unless they can be reduced to a common unit. For an open economy the same problem exists when workers produce goods for export and consume, in part, imported goods. Marx's theory of the wage (or value of labour-power) is something of a difficulty. He stated that the commodities needed by workers are not determined by purely physiological needs, though these set a minimum, but also contain a 'historical and moral' element. In other parts of his work, notably the pamphlet *Wage, Price and Profit,* there are elements of a theory of the determination of wages by bargaining power. What is clear is that if wages rise so far as to reduce profits below some minimum level, there will be a cessation of production and a crisis. This sets an upper limit to wages which ensures the existence of profit. Capital, in this framework, is 'value in process', money or commodities being used to produce surplus value. An individual capitalist's wealth is first in the form of money, then of means of production and labour-power, then of the commodities produced, and finally in the form of money, from the sale of the product, ready to start the cycle again. (In practice these stages overlap.) Capital is defined by the cycle as a whole. In measuring the capital involved we count the value of money, work in progress, means of production and final commodities. This differs from the definition of capital used in non-Marxist economics in two ways: the latter is narrower, in only including means of production, but wider in including means of production regardless of the social context. For Marx wealth is only capital if it is used by capitalists to produce surplus value in a capitalist system. I shall use this definition throughout. To put it another way, conventional economics treats capital as a technical requirement of production. Marx saw it as a social relation which defines a specific *mode of production.* We should pause here to consider the status of the two 'spheres' of *production* and *circulation* (exchange). Both are integral parts of the *circuit of capital,* the cycle described above. A capitalist economy consists of many separate enterprises, each controlled by a capitalist owner, linked together by market exchange, which is not controlled by anyone; capitalist production is anarchic and is governed by the blind working of economic laws independent of the will of any individual. The circuits of different capitals intertwine with each other: each buys means of production from others, while workers by means of subsistence from one capitalist with wages paid by another. Capitalist production as a whole includes many separate production processes and the processes of exchange that link them. Both are integral parts of production as a social process. Some Marxists have tried to argue that production (narrowly defined) is in some sense the primary element and circulation secondary. In view of the discussion Above, this view will not stand up. It is possible for part of production to be carried out under capitalist relations of production and part under pre-capitalist relations, linked by exchange, as in the relation between slave plantations in America and the Lancashire cotton textile industry at the time of the industrial revolution. Some writers describe this as wholly capitalist production (with an unorthodox form of labour discipline on the plantations), others as a relationship between two different modes of production. The question seems, at least in part, semantic. The important point is that there is a social process of production encompassing both capitalist and pre-capitalist relations of production, an important possibility in systems of commodity production. This, however, is to jump ahead; my concern at the moment is with a wholly capitalist system. The essential character of a capitalist system comes out most clearly in Marx's discussion of the *reproduction* of the system. For simplicity, he used the device of *simple reproduction,* in which the system is reconstituted exactly as before after each cycle of production, before moving on to *reproduction on an extended scale* (also called expanded reproduction, reproduction on a progressively increasing scale, and so on), where part of profit is accumulated, as new capital, and the system grows. Note also that the idea of a simple 'period of production', starting with means of production, wage goods for workers' consumption, and so on, and ending when they have been used up and replaced by newly produced goods, is another analytical fiction which simplifies the story without affecting the principles involved.

Consider first the relation between workers and capital. At the start of a period of production, workers have no wealth, 'nothing to sell but their labour-power', and therefore have no option but to look for a job. They cannot produce on their own account, since they cannot afford to buy means of production. The capitalist pays them a wage, enough to cover their (socially determined) needs. At the end of the period of production the workers have spent their wages, and are back where they started, forced once again to seek a job. Throughout, Marx assumed that there is a *reserve army of labour,* a pool of unemployed workers competing for jobs and keeping wages down. If expansion of the system absorbs all these unemployed workers, the threat of unemployment no longer holds down wages and maintains labour discipline; a crisis follows, reducing production, promoting labour-saving investment, and reconstituting the reserve army. Capitalists, on the other hand, start with purchasing power (*money capital*) sufficient to pay wages (*variable capital*) and buy means of production (*constant capital*). At the end of the process they get enough revenue to replace the outlay, plus a surplus (profit), which can be used entirely for their own consumption (simple reproduction) or partly for new investment (expanded reproduction). Starting, then, from a situation in which owners of commodities (capitalists) confront property less workers, the cycle of production ends with the reproduction of the same confrontation between the same two classes, ready for the cycle to start again. Where capitalism came from in the first place, is a different question, to be taken up later. To ensure the reproduction of the system, it is not enough that capitalists should get surplus value. Capitalism is a species of commodity production, so production is carried out by many separate capitals with no central co-coordinating plan. The right mix of use values (means of production, necessities of consumption and so on) must be produced. Marx analyzed this problem in the final chapters of *Capital* II, in terms of the exchange between two *departments* of social production: department 1, industries producing means of production; and department , producing consumer goods. He showed, using numerical examples, or *schemes of reproduction,* that there is a certain relation between the outputs of the two departments consistent with simple reproduction, and another relation, depending on the rate of accumulation, consistent with extended reproduction. It is easy to see how this analysis could be pursued in more detail to determine the necessary proportions between different branches of production within each department. One aspect of Marx's analysis of reproduction which is very relevant to the theory of imperialism and which has caused endless debate is the question of markets. How can capitalists hope to sell all the goods they produce? There is an argument used by many Marxist theorists, which I shall label *under-consumptions* (see Blamey 1976; a number of variants of under-consumptions will be discussed in later chapters, especially chapters 4, 7 and 8). In its simplest form it goes like this: if the workers cannot afford to buy the whole product, who can the capitalists sell it to? In simple reproduction, Marx's answer was that the capitalists consume the surplus product themselves. This entails selling to each other, since each specializes in the production of a particular product, but wishes to consume others. In a growing economy, capitalists still exchange the surplus product among them, but buy means of production for new investment instead of means of consumption, and the proportions between the two departments, 1 and 2, must be correspondingly different. The argument is slightly complicated by the assumption that wages are paid in advance; some of the new investment takes the form of wage payments to additional workers, who spend the money on consumer goods. The money used to carry out transactions is not a problem either, since it passes from hand to hand without being used up. At the end of each cycle it has returned to its starting point, ready to circulate again. The core idea of under-consumptions is that consumer demand is somehow more fundamental than demand for means of production, that the latter only exists to provide for the former. It is often argued (Hobson 1938, is a classic case) that if consumption is (say) static; because wages are constant, then there will be no incentive to invest. This is simply wrong, since investment can be directed to industries producing investment goods (means of production) as well as to the consumer goods industries. Consumer demand has no special status in a capitalist framework; the bulk of it is from workers, who will only be employed if they contribute to profits, so both consumption and investment derive primarily from Profit-seeking decisions by capitalists. If capitalists save and invest, more workers are needed, and total workers' consumption goes up. (Bernstein).

It is possible that investment will be insufficient if profit prospects are poor. In this case, capitalists cut back on investment and employment, reducing demand and setting off a chain reaction. On the other hand, when high profits are expected, the chain reaction works the other way round. Marx expected capitalism to evolve through a series of booms (which ensure the development of the forces of production) and slumps, or 'periodic crises'. The schemes of expanded reproduction show that it is possible in principle for demand to expand in line with supply, though it is equally possible for the system to suffer crises (as it does in practice). The explanation of crises must be sought in the determinants of profitability, not in any inherent problem of demand. I shall discuss particular variants of under-consumptions as they arise, notably those of Luxemburg, Hobson, and Sweeny. Under-consumptions arguments are important in the theory of imperialism because they can explain a search for external markets to make up for the deficiency of demand at home.

The Experience of 1848-51

The Eve of Revolution

The first works of mature Marxism-*The Poverty of Philosophy* and the *Communist Manifesto-* appeared just on the eve of the revolution of 1848. For this reason, in addition to presenting the general principles of Marxism, they reflect to a certain degree the concrete revolutionary situation of the time. It wills, therefore, be more expedient, perhaps, to examine what the authors of these works said about the state immediately before they drew conclusions from the experience of the years 1848-51.

In The Poverty of Philosophy, Marx Wrote

"The working class, in the course of development, will substitute for the old bourgeois society an association which will preclude classes and their antagonism, and there will be no more political power groups, since the political power is precisely the official expression of class antagonism in bourgeois society." It is instructive to compare this general exposition of the idea of the state disappearing after the abolition of classes with the exposition contained in the *Communist Manifesto*, written by Marx and Engels a few months later in November 1847, to be exact: "In depicting the most general phases of the development of the proletariat, we traced the more or less veiled civil war, raging within existing society up to the point where that war breaks out into open revolution, and where the violent overthrow of the bourgeoisie lays the foundation for the sway of the proletariat.... "... We have seen above that the first step in the revolution by the working class is to raise the proletariat to the position of the ruling class to win the battle of democracy. "The proletariat will use its political supremacy to wrest, by degree, all capital from the bourgeoisie, to centralize all instruments of production in the hands of the state, i.e., of the proletariat organized as the ruling class; and to increase the total productive forces as rapidly as possible." Here we have a formulation of one of the most remarkable and most important ideas of Marxism on the subject of the state, namely, the idea of the "dictatorship of the proletariat" (as Marx and Engels began to call it after the Paris Commune); And, also, a highly interesting definition of the state, which is also one of the "forgotten words" of Marxism: "the state, i.e., the proletariat organized as the ruling class." This definition of the state has never been explained in the prevailing propaganda and agitation literature of the official Social Democratic parties. More than that, it has been deliberately ignored, for it is absolutely irreconcilable with reformism, and is a slap in the face for the common opportunist prejudices and philistine illusions about the "peaceful development of democracy". The proletariat needs the state-this is repeated by all the opportunists, social chauvinists and Kautskyites, who assure us that this is what Marx taught. But they "forget" to add that, in the first place, according to Marx, the proletariat needs only a state which is withering away, i.e., a state so constituted that it begins to wither away immediately, and cannot but wither away. And, secondly, the working people need a "state, i.e., the proletariat organized as the ruling class". The state is a special organization of force: it is an organization of violence for the suppression of some class. What class must the proletariat suppress? Naturally, only the exploiting class, i.e., the bourgeoisie. The working people need the state only to suppress the resistance of the exploiters, and only the proletariat can direct this suppression, can carry it out. For the proletariat is the only class that is consistently revolutionary, the only class that can unite all the working and exploited people in the struggle against the bourgeoisie, in completely removing it. The exploiting classes need political rule to maintain exploitation, i.e., in the selfish interests of an insignificant minority against the vast majority of all people. The exploited classes need political rule in order to completely abolish all exploitation, i.e., in the interests of the vast majority of the people, and against the insignificant minority consisting of the modern slave-owners the landowners and capitalists.(Brewer)

The petty bourgeois democrats, those sham socialists who replaced the class struggle by dreams of class harmony, even pictured the socialist transformation in a dreamy fashion not as the overthrow of the rule of the exploiting class, but as the peaceful submission of the minority to the majority which has become aware of its aims. This petty bourgeois utopia, which is inseparable from the idea of the state being above classes, led in practice to the betrayal of the interests of the working classes, as was shown, for example, by the history of the French revolutions of 1848 and 1871, and by the experience of "socialist" participation in Bourgeois Cabinets in Britain, France, Italy and other countries at the turn of the century.

All his life Marx fought against this petty bourgeois socialism, now revived in Russia by the Socialist Revolutionary and Menshevik parties. He developed his theory of the class struggle consistently, down to the theory of political power, of the state. The overthrow of bourgeois rule can be accomplished only by the proletariat, the particular class whose economic conditions of existence prepare it for this task and provide it with the possibility and the power to perform it. While the bourgeoisie break up and disintegrate the peasantry and all the petty bourgeois

Groups, they weld together, unite and organize the proletariat. Only the proletariat-by virtue of the economic role it plays in large-scale production is capable of being the leader of all the working and exploited people, whom the bourgeoisie exploit, oppress and crush, often not less but more than they do the proletarians, but who are incapable of waging an independent struggle for their emancipation.

The theory of class struggle, applied by Marx to the question of the state and the socialist revolution, leads as a matter of course to the recognition of the political rule of the proletariat, of its dictatorship, i.e., undivided power directly backed by the armed force of the people. The overthrow of the bourgeoisie can be achieved only by the proletariat becoming the ruling class, capable of crushing the inevitable and desperate resistance of the bourgeoisie, and of organizing all the working and exploited people for the new economic system. The proletariat needs state power, a centralized organization of force, an organization of violence, both to crush the resistance of the exploiters and to lead the enormous mass of the population the peasants, the petty bourgeoisie, and semi proletarians in the work of organizing a socialist economy. By educating the workers' party, Marxism educates the vanguard of the proletariat, capable of assuming power and leading the whole people to socialism, of directing and organizing the new system, of being the teacher, the guide, the leader of all the working and exploited people in organizing their social life without the bourgeoisie and against the bourgeoisie. By contrast, the opportunism now prevailing trains the members of the workers' party to be the representatives of the better paid workers, who lose touch with the masses, "get along" fairly well under capitalism, and sell their birthright for a mess of pottage, i.e., renounce their role as revolutionary leaders of the people against the bourgeoisie. Marx's theory of "the state, i.e., the proletariat organized as the ruling class", is inseparably bound up with the whole of his doctrine of the revolutionary role of the proletariat in history. The culmination of this rule is the proletarian dictatorship, the political rule of the proletariat. "This executive power with its enormous bureaucratic and military organization, with its vast and ingenious state machinery, with a host of officials numbering half a million, besides an army of another half million, this appalling parasitic body, which enmeshes the body of French society and chokes all its pores, sprang up in the days of the absolute monarchy, with the decay of the feudal system, which it helped to hasten." The first French Revolution developed centralization, "but at the same time" it increased "the extent, the attributes and the number of agents of governmental power. Napoleon completed this state machinery". The legitimate monarchy and the July monarchy "added nothing but a greater division of labor" Finally, in its struggle against the revolution, the parliamentary republic found itself compelled to strengthen, along with repressive measures, the resources and centralization of governmental power. All revolutions perfected this machine instead of smashing it. The parties that contended in turn for domination regarded the possession of this huge state edifice as the principal spoils of the victor." (*The Eighteenth Brumaire of Louis Bonaparte* pp.1899, fourth In this remarkable argument, Marxism takes a tremendous step forward compared with the *Communist Manifesto*) In the latter, the question of the state is still treated in an extremely abstract manner, in the most general terms and expressions. In the above quoted passage, the question is treated in a concrete manner, and the conclusion is extremely precise, definite, practical and palpable: all previous revolutions perfected the state machine, whereas it must be broken, smashed. This conclusion is the chief and fundamental point in the Marxist theory of the state. And it is precisely this fundamental point which has been completely ignored by the dominant official Social Democratic parties and, indeed, distorted (as we shall see later) by the foremost theoretician of the Second International, Karl Kautsky. The *Communist Manifesto* gives a general summary of history, which compels us to regard the state as the organ of class rule and leads us to the inevitable conclusion that the proletariat cannot overthrow the bourgeoisie without first winning political power, without attaining political supremacy, without transforming the state into the "proletariat organized as the ruling class"; And that this proletarian state will begin to wither away immediately after its victory because the state is unnecessary and cannot exist in a society in which there are no class antagonisms. The question as to how, from the point of view of historical development, the replacement of the bourgeois by the proletarian state is to take place is not raised here. This is the question Marx raises and answers in 1852. True to his philosophy of dialectical materialism, Marx takes as his basis the historical experience of the great years of revolution, 1848 to 1851. Here, as everywhere else, his theory is a summing up of experience, illuminated by a profound philosophical conception of the world and a rich knowledge of history.

The issue of the state is put specifically: How did the bourgeois state, the state machine necessary for the rule of the bourgeoisie, come into being historically? What changes did it undergo, what evolution did it perform in the course of bourgeois revolutions and in the face of the independent actions of the oppressed classes? What are the tasks of the proletariat in relation to this state machine? The centralized state power that is peculiar to bourgeois society came into being in the period of the fall of absolutism. Two institutions most characteristic of this state machine are the bureaucracy and the standing army. In their works, Marx and Engels repeatedly show that the bourgeoisie are connected with these institutions by thousands of threads. Every worker's experience illustrates this connection in an extremely graphic and impressive manner. From its own bitter experience, the working class learns to recognize this connection. That is why it so easily grasps and so firmly learns the doctrine which shows the inevitability of this connection, a doctrine which the petty bourgeois democrats either ignorantly and flippantly deny, or still more flippantly admit "in general", while forgetting to draw appropriate practical conclusions. The bureaucracy and the standing army are a "parasite" on the body of bourgeois society a parasite created by the internal antagonisms which rend that society, but a parasite which "chokes" all its vital pores. The Kautskyite opportunism now prevailing in official Social Democracy considers the view that the state is a parasitic organism to be the peculiar and exclusive attribute of anarchism. It goes without saying that this distortion of Marxism is of vast advantage to those philistines who have reduced socialism to the unheard of disgrace of justifying and prettifying the imperialist war by applying to it the concept of "defense of the fatherland"; but it is unquestionably a distortion, nevertheless. The development, perfection, and strengthening of the bureaucratic and military apparatus proceeded during all the numerous bourgeois revolutions which Europe has witnessed since the fall of feudalism. In particular, it is the petty bourgeois who are attracted to the side of the big bourgeoisie and are largely subordinated to them through this apparatus, which provides the upper sections of the peasants, small artisans, tradesmen, and the like with comparatively comfortable, quiet, and respectable jobs raising the holders above the people. Consider what happened in Russia during the six months following February 27, 1917. The official posts which formerly were given by preference to the Black Hundreds have now become the spoils of the Cadets, Mensheviks, and Social Revolutionaries. Nobody has really thought of introducing any serious reforms. Every effort has been made to put them off "until the Constituent Assembly meets", and to steadily put off its convocation until after the war! But there has been no delay, no waiting for the Constituent Assembly, in the matter of dividing the spoils of getting the lucrative jobs of ministers, deputy ministers, governors general, etc., etc.! The game of combinations that has been played in forming the government has been, in essence, only an expression of this division and red vision of the "spoils", which has been going on above and below, throughout the country, in every department of central and local government. The distribution of official jobs accomplished and "mistakes" in the distribution corrected by a few redistributions. But the more the bureaucratic apparatus is "redistributed" among the various bourgeois and petty bourgeois parties (among the Cadets,

Socialist Revolutionaries and Mensheviks in the case of Russia), the more keenly aware the oppressed classes, and the proletariat at their head, become of their irreconcilable hostility to the whole of bourgeois society. Hence the need for all bourgeois parties, even for the most democratic and "revolutionary democratic" among them, to intensify repressive measures against the revolutionary proletariat, to strengthen the apparatus of coercion, i.e., the state machine. This course of events compels the revolution "to concentrate all its forces of destruction" against the state power, and to set itself the aim, not of improving the state machine, but of smashing and destroying it. It was not logical reasoning, but actual developments, the actual experience of 184851, that led to the matter being presented in this way. The extent to which Marx held strictly to the solid ground of historical experience can be seen from the fact that, in 1852, he did not yet specifically raise the question of what was to take the place of the state machine to be destroyed. Experience had not yet provided material for dealing With this question, which history placed on the agenda later on, in 1871. In 1852, all that could be established with the accuracy of scientific observation was that the proletarian revolution had approached the task of "concentrating all its forces of destruction" against the state power, of "smashing" the state machine. Here the question may arise: is it correct to generalize the experience, observations and conclusions of Marx, to apply them to a field that is wider than the history of France during the three years 184851? Before proceeding to deal with this question, let us recall a remark made by Engels and then examine the facts. In his introduction to the third edition of *The Eighteenth Brumaire*, Engels wrote: "France is the country where, more than anywhere else, the historical class struggles were each time fought out to a finish, and where, consequently, the changing political forms within which they move and in which their results are summarized have been stamped in the sharpest outlines. The centre of feudalism in the Middle Ages, the model country, since the Renaissance, of a unified monarchy based on social estates, France demolished feudalism in the Great Revolution and established the rule of the bourgeoisie in a classical purity unequalled by any other European land. And the struggle of the upward striving proletariat against the ruling bourgeoisie appeared here in an acute form unknown elsewhere." The last remark is out of date insomuch as since 1871 there has been a lull in the revolutionary struggle of the French proletariat, although, long as this lull may be, it does not at all preclude the possibility that in the coming proletarian revolution France may show herself to be the classic country of the class struggle to a finish. Let us, however, cast a general glance over the history of the advanced countries at the turn of the century. We shall see that the same process went on more slowly, in more varied forms, in a much wider field: on the one hand, the development of "parliamentary power" both in the republican countries (France, America, Switzerland), and in the monarchies (Britain, Germany to a certain extent, Italy, the Scandinavia countries, etc.); on the other hand, a struggle for power among the various bourgeois and petty bourgeois parties which distributed and redistributed the "spoils" of office, with the foundations of bourgeois society unchanged; and, lastly, the perfection and consolidation of the "executive power", of its bureaucratic and military apparatus.

There is not the slightest doubt that these features are common to the whole of the modern evolution of all capitalist states in general. In the last three years 1848-51 France displayed, in a swift, sharp, concentrated form, the very same processes of development which are peculiar to the whole capitalist world. Imperialism the era of bank capital, the era of gigantic capitalist monopolies, of the development of monopoly capitalism into state monopoly capitalism has clearly shown an unprecedented growth in its bureaucratic and military apparatus in connection with the intensification of repressive measures against the proletariat both in the monarchical and in the freest, republican countries.

World history is now undoubtedly leading, on an incomparably larger scale than in 1852, to the "concentration of all the forces" of the proletarian revolution on the "destruction" of the state machine. What the proletariat will put in its place is suggested by the highly instructive material furnished by the Paris Commune.

Experience of the Paris Commune of 1871. Marx's Analysis

It is well known that in the autumn of 1870, a few months before the Commune, Marx warned the Paris workers that any attempt to overthrow the government would be the folly of despair. But when, in March 1871, a decisive battle was forced upon the workers and they accepted it, when the uprising had become a fact, Marx greeted the proletarian revolution with the greatest enthusiasm, in spite of unfavorable auguries. Marx did not persist in the pedantic attitude of condemning an "untimely" movement as did the ill famed Russian renegade from Marxism, Plekhanov, who in November 1905 wrote encouragingly about the workers' and peasants' struggle, but after December 1905 cried, liberal fashion: "They should not have taken up arms." Marx, however, was not only enthusiastic about the heroism of the Communards, who, as he expressed it, "stormed heaven". Although the mass revolutionary movement did not achieve its aim, he regarded it as a historic experience of enormous importance, as a certain advance of the world proletarian revolution, as a practical step that was more important than hundreds of programmes and arguments. Marx endeavored to analyze this experiment, to draw tactical lessons from it and reexamine his theory in the light of it.

Controversy with the Anarchists

This controversy took place in 1873. Marx and Engels contributed articles against the Proudhonists, "autonomists" or "antiauthoritarians", to an Italian socialist annual, and it was not until 1913 that these articles appeared in German in Neue Zeit.

"If the political struggle of the working class assumes revolutionary form," wrote Marx, ridiculing the anarchists for their repudiation of politics, "and if the workers set up their revolutionary dictatorship in place of the dictatorship of the bourgeoisie, they commit the terrible crime of violating principles, for in order to satisfy their wretched, vulgar everyday needs and to crush the resistance of the bourgeoisie, they give the state a revolutionary and transient form, instead of laying down their arms and abolishing the state." It was solely against this kind of "abolition" of the state that Marx fought in refuting the anarchists! He did not at all oppose the view that the state would disappear when classes disappeared, or that it would be abolished when classes were abolished. What he did oppose was the proposition that the workers should renounce the use of arms, organized violence, that is, the state, which is to serve to "crush the resistance of the bourgeoisie". To prevent the true meaning of his struggle against anarchism from being distorted, Marx expressly emphasized the "revolutionary and transient form" of the state which the proletariat needs. The proletariat needs the state only temporarily. We do not after all differ with the anarchists on the question of the abolition of the state as the aim. We maintain that, to achieve this aim, we must temporarily make use of the instruments, resources, and methods of state power against the exploiters, just as the temporary dictatorship of the oppressed class is necessary for the abolition of classes. The usual criticism of anarchism by present day Social Democrats has boiled down to the purest philistine banality: "We recognize the state, whereas the anarchists do not!" Naturally, such banality cannot but repel workers who are at all capable of thinking and revolutionary minded. What Engels says is different. He stresses that all socialists recognize that the state will disappear as a result of the socialist revolution. He then deals specifically with the question of the revolution the very question which, as a rule, the Social Democrats evade out of opportunism, leaving it, so to speak, exclusively for the anarchists "to work out". Prevailing official Social Democracy usually dismissed the question of the concrete tasks of the proletariat in the revolution either with a philistine sneer, or, at best, with the sophistic evasion: "The future will show". And the anarchists were justified in saying about such Social Democrats that they were failing in their task of giving the workers a revolutionary education. Engels draws upon the experience of the last proletarian revolution precisely for the purpose of making a most concrete study of what should be done by the proletariat, and in what manner, in relation to both the banks and the state.

Engels wrote to Bebel criticizing the same draft of the Gotha Programme which Marx criticized in his famous letter to Bracke. Referring specially to the question of the state, Engels said: "The free people's state has been transferred into the free state. Taken in its grammatical sense, a free state is one where the state is free in relation to its citizens, hence a state with a despotic government. The whole talk about the state should be dropped, especially since the Commune, which was no longer a state in the proper sense of the word. The 'people's state' has been thrown in our faces by the anarchists to the point of disgust, although already Marx's book against Proudhon and later the *Communist Manifesto* say plainly that with the introduction of the socialist order of society the state dissolves of itself [sich auflost] and disappears. As the state is only a transitional institution which is used in the struggle, in the revolution, to hold down one's adversaries by force, it is sheer nonsense to talk of a 'free people's state'; so long as the proletariat still needs the state, it does not need it in the interests of freedom but in order to hold down its adversaries, and as soon as it becomes possible to speak of freedom the state as such ceases to exist. We would therefore propose replacing the state everywhere by Gemeinwesen, a good old German word which can very well take the place of the French word commune." (pp.321-22 of the German original.)

The Transition from Capitalism to Communism

Marx has continued; "Between capitalist and communist society lies the period of the revolutionary transformation of the one into the other. Corresponding to this is also a political transition period in which the state can be nothing but the revolutionary dictatorship of the proletariat."Marx bases this conclusion on an analysis of the role played by the proletariat in modern capitalist society, on the data concerning the development of this society, and on the irreconcilability of the antagonistic interests of the proletariat and the bourgeoisie.

Previously the question was put as follows: to achieve its emancipation, the proletariat must overthrow the bourgeoisie, win political power and establish its revolutionary dictatorship. Now the question is put somewhat differently: the transition from capitalist society which is developing towards communism to communist society is impossible without a "political transition period", and the state in this period can only be the revolutionary dictatorship of the proletariat.

We have seen that the *Communist Manifesto* simply places side by side the two concepts: "to raise the proletariat to the position of the ruling class" and "to win the battle of democracy". On the basis of all that has been said above, it is possible to determine more precisely how democracy changes in the transition from capitalism to communism. In capitalist society, providing it develops under the most favourable conditions, we have a more or less complete democracy in the democratic republic. But this democracy is always hemmed in by the narrow limits set by capitalist exploitation, and consequently always remains, in effect, a democracy for the minority, only for the propertied classes, only for the rich. Freedom in capitalist society always remains about the same as it was in the ancient Greek republics: freedom for the slave-owners. Owing to the conditions of capitalist exploitation, the modern wage slaves are so crushed by want and poverty that "they cannot be bothered with democracy", "cannot be bothered with politics"; in the ordinary, peaceful course of events, the majority of the population is debarred from participation in public and political life. The correctness of this statement is perhaps most clearly confirmed by Germany, because constitutional legality steadily endured there for a remarkably long time nearly half a century (1871-1914) and during this period the Social Democrats were able to achieve far more than in other countries in the way of "utilizing legality", and organized a larger proportion of the workers into a political party than anywhere else in the world.

Marx grasped this essence of capitalist democracy splendidly when, in analyzing the experience of the Commune, he said that the oppressed are allowed once every few years to decide which particular representatives of the oppressing class shall represent and repress them in parliament!

But from this capitalist democracy that is inevitably narrow and stealthily pushes aside the poor, and is therefore hypocritical and false through and through forward development does not proceed simply, directly and smoothly, towards "greater and greater democracy", as the liberal professors and petty bourgeois opportunists would have us believe. No, forward development, i.e., development towards communism, proceeds through the dictatorship of the proletariat, and cannot do otherwise, for the resistance of the capitalist exploiters cannot be broken by anyone else or in any other way. And the dictatorship of the proletariat, i.e., the organization of the vanguard of the oppressed as the ruling class for the purpose of suppressing the oppressors, cannot result merely in an expansion of democracy.

Simultaneously with an immense expansion of democracy, which for the first time becomes democracy for? The poor, democracy for the people, and not democracy for the moneybags, the dictatorship of the proletariat imposes a series of restrictions on the freedom of the oppressors, the exploiters, the capitalists. We must suppress them in order to free humanity from wage slavery, their resistance must be crushed by force; it is clear that there is no freedom and no democracy where there is suppression and where there is violence. Engels expressed this splendidly in his letter to Bebel when he said, as the reader will remember, that "the proletariat needs the state, not in the interests of freedom but in order to hold down its adversaries, and as soon as it becomes possible to speak of freedom the state as such ceases to exist". Democracy for the vast majority of the people, and suppression by force, i.e., exclusion from democracy, of the exploiters and oppressors of the people this is the change democracy undergoes during the transition from capitalism to communism. Only in communist society, when the resistance of the capitalists have disappeared, when there are no classes (i.e., when there is no distinction between the members of society as regards their relation to the social means of production), only then "the state... ceases to exist", and "it becomes possible to speak of freedom". Only then will a truly complete democracy become possible and be realized, a democracy without any exceptions whatever. And only then will democracy begin to wither away, owing to the simple fact that, freed from capitalist slavery, from the untold horrors, savagery, absurdities, and infamies of capitalist exploitation, people will gradually become accustomed to observing the elementary rules of social intercourse that have been known for centuries and repeated for thousands of years in all copybook maxims. They will become accustomed to observing them without force, without coercion, without subordination, without the special apparatus for coercion called the state. The expression "the state withers away" is very well chosen, for it indicates both the gradual and the spontaneous nature of the process. Only habit can, and undoubtedly will, have such an effect; for we see around us on millions of occasions how readily people become accustomed to observing the necessary rules of social intercourse when there is no exploitation, when there is nothing that arouses indignation, evokes protest and revolt, and creates the need for suppression.

Lenin in his *The Development of Capitalism in Russia* (1893) showed that capitalism was developing in Russia.

In 1900 the Russian Social Democratic Labour Party was formed. Within the party there were three different views as to how the movement should unfold.

1. The Menshevik view- they argued that Marx had seen capitalism as being the next stage after feudalism because it was capitalism that would develop the productive forces to the level that would make socialism possible. Therefore the worker's movement should support the bourgeoisie to take power.
2. The Bolshevik view- They agreed but believed that the bourgeoisie would not do it of its own accord. The workers and peasants must take power on their behalf but only to put capitalism on the agenda and to do away with feudalism.

3. The view of Trotsky- After the failed revolution of 1905 Trotsky developed the theory of permanent revolution which argued that the workers must lead the peasants against feudalism but that they will not stop at the tasks that one normally associates with capitalism (such as land reform and the abolition of feudal rule) but will proceed directly to socialism as the first stage of world revolution. He argued that in the era of imperialism that there are no stages and that nations will not mechanically repeat the evolution of centuries past.

Lenin came to the same position once he arrived back in Russia in April 1917.

The R.S.D.L.P. formed in 1900 but in 1903 there was a split between the Mensheviks (meaning minority in Russian) and the Bolsheviks (meaning majority in Russian) on the question, amongst others, of who should be a member of the party.

The Mensheviks wanted all who agreed with the programme of the party to be members but the Bolsheviks wanted a party of active professional revolutionaries in a party using the principles of "democratic centralism." This was not the bureaucratic centralism in fact practiced under Stalin in the name of "democratic centralism." Rather it meant the greatest democracy possible in the party in the making of decisions combined with complete unity in action (See *what is to be done* by V.I. Lenin)

Chapter - III

Idealistic Concept on Marxism, Leninism and Capitalism

Marx, Engels and Lenin on the British Workers' Movement

We speak loosely of the Chartist "movement," but few of us look on Chartism as a movement; that is, as a developing class struggle having definite origins, having relations to the changing class conditions of the England of that day, having definite aims. Yet this was precisely how Marx and Engels regarded Chartism.

They themselves were "Chartists." Their own political tactics they based largely on the experience of the Chartists. They studied every development of Chartism, had opinions on every Chartist leader. Yet no one has ever troubled to find out what were the ideas of the founders of revolutionary Communism upon revolutionary Chartism and its leaders. Indeed, in our press, in our literature we find ideas which are absolutely the opposite of those of Marx and Engels on Chartism.

Engels, who from the end of 1842 was closely connected with the Chartists, saw the movement in its beginning as a revolutionary democratic movement, the natural development of the Radical movement of 1793 to 1799, which developed on a mass scale at the close of the war with France in 1815.

The English working class was the best organized the most advanced in Europe. If the six demands of its Charter were those of the democratic revolution and not of the social revolution, the workers were not long in making it clear that they were fighting for the democratic revolution, not in order to pull chestnuts out of the fire for a cowardly bourgeoisie, but in order to establish themselves, the workers, as the ruling class in order to start the social revolution. The day had passed when the democratic revolution could be realized in England without leading directly to the emancipation of the proletariat.

"The whole struggle of the workers against the factory owners," writes Marx in 1848, "which has already lasted eighty years, a struggle which began with machine-breaking and then went through the stages of combinations, separate attacks on the persons and property of factory-owners and the few workers devoted to the factory-owners, through more or less big revolts, through the insurrections of 1839 and 1842, has developed into the most conscious class struggle which the world has ever seen the whole of this class struggle of the Chartists, the organized party of the proletariat, against the organized State power of the bourgeoisie is a social civil war."

A little earlier Marx had written that in the Chartists the workers had formed a political party whose fighting slogan could in no case merely be "monarchy or republic?" but "the rule of the working class or the rule of the bourgeoisie?"

At this time all the political efforts of the bourgeoisie were concentrated on winning free trade through the repeal of the Corn Laws. The Chartists, the real banner-bearers of the democratic revolution, were never for a moment deceived by the efforts of their class enemies to draw them into this "fight for freedom." They fought equally hard on two fronts against both the free trade exploiters and the protectionist exploiters. The Chartists forced the Corn Law Leaguers to hold their meetings by ticket in guarded halls, drove them off the streets and out of their press. They ironically compared their liberal words with their reactionary practice. "Everyone knows," Marx said, "that in England the struggle between Liberals and Democrats takes the name of the struggle between Free Traders and Chartists."

What were the personal relations of Marx and Engels to the leaders of Chartism? Max Beer and Rothstein would have us believe they were quite uncritical, or that where they criticized they were wrong. Groves follows them in making idols of Harney and Jones, while J. P. Lilburne accepts the Beer-Rothstein estimate of O'Brien.

O'Connor they rightly considered a brilliant agitator and journalist, but his political role was reactionary. "A true representative of old England. By his nature he is conservative and fosters a fully determined hatred both to industrial progress and to revolution. All his ideas are thoroughly permeated with a patriarchal petty-bourgeois spirit." O'Connor in many ways resembled Cobbett. He represented the revolt of the dying hand-weaver, or pre-industrial-revolution England against the triumph of the new industrial bourgeoisie.

O'Brien, the other petty-bourgeois Chartist leader, Marx and Engels always considered the least talented of the Chartists. Engels told Belfort Bax that O'Brien's *Rise, Progress and Phases of Human Slavery* was the least valuable production of the whole movement. As a politician O'Brien was beneath contempt, moved by personal spites and intrigues and even in his best period, that of the first Convention, having no fixed policy. He was a Roman Catholic, a currency crank and land reformer. His followers in the First International, who believed in land nationalization, were sometimes used by Marx as a counter to the trade union element. Some O'Brienites survived into the S.D.F., and Hyndman praised them extravagantly. His ideas on the class struggle were only those of the Chartist movement in general and had no particular influence on Marx and Engels.

Harney, who was a real revolutionary and a close collaborator of Marx and Engels, was also judged by them very critically. Once even they called him, not without reason, "a lousy little fellow." Harney was something of a phraseur. He never took the leading part in the Chartist movement his abilities entitled him to, and he lacked political sense. After 1848 he became a worshipper of Louis Blanc, and in a few years had become a petty-bourgeois radical. He sent a subscription to the First International, but never worked for it.

Ernest Jones was a man of more serious caliber. In 1848 and later Marx and Engels saw in him the leader of the English workers. When ten years later he gave up the struggle Marx wrote to Weider meyer, "Imagine an army whose general on the day of battle deserts to the enemy." He never wrote with such bitterness of Harney, for Harney's desertion was of less importance. Even after Jones in 1859 became a Radical Engels continued his friend. He refused to join the International but asked for its support in his election at Manchester. "One more of the old guard," Marx wrote sadly on his death. "Certainly his bourgeois phrases were only hypocrisy," Engels wrote in answer. "Here in Manchester there is no one to replace him among the workers . He was the only EDUCATED Englishman among the politicians who stood fully on our side."

Jones, they knew, "was no Harney." He was the greatest leader the English workers produced in the nineteenth century, and it is not without significance that he was also the most revolutionary, the most Marxist. He was broken by circumstance and by his own ambition, but to the end remained an honest man, respected even by those he had betrayed. Marx would not speak at the memorial meeting arranged by the Reform League in 1869 in Trafalgar Square, but he nevertheless bitterly regretted the loss of Jones.

There are many lessons to be learned to-day from a Marxist estimate of the Chartist movement of the past, its class relationships, its mistakes, its triumphs. There is nothing to be gained by concealing the Marxist viewpoint, either on the movement as a whole or its different leaders.

Marx and Engels did not live to see the epoch of imperialism, but Lenin, who applied Marxism to the study of the problems of imperialism, the last stage of capitalism, very carefully studied all they had written about the English workers. The indications given by Marx and Engels as to the development of the English proletarian under monopoly conditions, the buying over of the upper section of the "Labour aristocracy," the creation of "a bourgeois Labour Party" (the old trade union movement of Burt, MacDonald, Shipton, etc.), gave Lenin valuable ideas as to the development of the working class as a whole in conditions of monopoly capitalism, of imperialism.

More than this, between 1908 and 1914, when the war finally split the Labour movement in Europe, Lenin closely followed the development of the English workers, noting every sign of a revolt against opportunism. Engels's struggle with Hyndman he approved to the last word, noting after Engels's death how the S.D.F. continued by its policy to justify Engels's position.

The crime of the S.D.F., and of the S.D.P. and B.S.P. which followed it, was that they made of Marxism a dogma instead of a guide to action, to practical activity; that they did not know how "to penetrate into the unconscious but powerful class instinct of the trade unions." The creation of the Labour Party, with which the S.D.F. refused to affiliate, was a great step forward in the mass organization of the British workers. At the same time Lenin points out it would have been a mistake to consider the Labour Party as independent of the bourgeois parties, as carrying on the class struggle, as Socialist, etc.

The S.D.F. committed typical Left sectarian mistakes in their policy towards the Labour Party, while the I.L.P., on the other hand, behaved in a typically Right opportunist fashion in trying (and succeeding) to make the workers believe the Labour Party was a party of struggle, a Socialist party.

This brilliant characterization of the two wings of British social democracy Lenin gave in 1908. Three years later he was already able to notice a reflection of the growing class struggle in Britain in a revolt against the leadership of both parties.

At the Coventry Conference of the S.D.P. the Hackney Branch had a resolution condemning Hyndman's jingo "Big Navy" articles. Although the whole Executive defended Hyndman the resolution was only defeated by forcing a group vote in place of individual voting. At the Birmingham Conference of the I.L.P. a strong move was also made against the dependence of the Labour Party in Parliament on the Liberals.

Lenin here for the first time made his ironical comment on the I.L.P., that it is "independent of Socialism, dependent on Liberalism," and pointed out the tremendous importance a workers' daily might have for fighting opportunism. Next year the *Daily Herald* was started, but its opportunism was almost at once evident.

The *Daily Herald* hastened to declare in a leader that "we stand for absolute freedom of thought and action, freedom from any kind of party ties." "A Socialist paper," Lenin comments bitterly, *"disclaiming all party ties, you cannot find a better characterization of the pitiful condition of the political organization of the working class in England."*

But 1911 saw the great railway strike; 1912 the great miners' strike. The workers were learning to fight independently of all so-called leaders. A syndicalism movement—not very strong—began. In fright the bourgeoisie, led by Lloyd George, began to grant concessions they had never given to the Labour Party's "peaceful persuasion": a minimum wage for the miners, a plan for agrarian reform. It is true the concessions were worthless, but Lloyd George was a master showman and deceiver of the masses.

As a result of these great class movements changes again took place in the Social Democratic parties. At the Merthyr Congress of the I.L.P. in 1912 a demand was again made to break with the Liberals in Parliament. Keir Hardie and Snowden had the greatest difficulty in getting the resolution defeated. In the B.S.P., the rank-and-file delegates at the Black pool Conference in 1913 succeeded in decisively defeating Hyndman and the Executive Council on the Big Navy question. Only two of the old members were re-elected. This ability to throw overboard an "old-guard" leadership which had proved thoroughly opportunist in practice Lenin counted "a big plus for the English movement."

There is no need to deal with Lenin's relation to the English movement during and after the war. These things are well known, particularly his decisive part at the Second Congress of the Co intern in formulating the tactics of the newly formed British Communist Party. But it is important to remember that Lenin's tactic for the British workers was not something accidental; it was the development of views held for many years, firmly based on the teaching of Marx and Engels in regard to the British movement and developed to correspond to the conditions of imperialism. That movement Lenin had watched very carefully, knew thoroughly.

The British Communist Party is in no sense the "heir" of the old S.D.F., as some comrades would have us believe. It is in a much truer sense the heir of the Chartists, with almost a century of working-class experience to aid it in avoiding the mistakes of the Chartists, and having the advice and teaching of the three greatest teachers of the international working class to guide it, a teaching which developed continuously, from 1843 to Lenin's death in 1924, in unbroken living contact with the realities of the British situation.

The Origins of Capitalism

Capitalism, once in existence, has a logic which can be captured by abstract theory, but its origins are a once-for-all process that must be explained in terms of specific historical circumstances. Since the defining feature of capitalism, for Marx, is the relation between a class of property less, free workers, and a class of private owners of the means of production, the essence of the problem is to explain how these two classes came into being. Capitalism first emerged in Europe. It was transplanted, partly grown, to colonies of European settlement (America, Australia, etc.) and developed independently in Japan. In the rest of the world capitalism came from outside as an alien growth introduced frequently, at the point of a gun. Marx did not regard this geographical pattern as accidental. He argued that the prospects for the development of capitalism depended crucially on the previous structure of society, which differed in different parts of the world.

Europe (and Japan; *Capital* I, ch. 27: 718n) was dominated by the feudal mode of production, and most of Asia (particularly India and China) by the Asiatic mode of production. The decay of the feudal mode of production created a fertile environment for the growth of capitalism, while the Asiatic mode did not, because feudalism involved a form of private property inland (the main means of production in a principally agrarian society), while the Asiatic mode of production was based on communal ownership of land. 'Bernier correctly discovers the basic form of all phenomena in the East – he refers to Turkey, Persia, Hindustan to be the *absence of private property* in land.

This is the real key even to the Oriental heaven' (Marx 1969: 451). Since this aspect of Marx's thought is controversial, he quote here some extracts from *Capital* to demonstrate Marx's view of the importance of the pre-existing social structure in determining the prospects for the development of capitalism. Usury has a revolutionary effect in all precapitalist modes of production only in so far as it destroys and dissolves those forms of property on whose solid foundation and continual reproduction in the same form the political organisation is based. Under Asian forms, usury can continue a long time, without producing anything more than economic decay and political corruption. Only where and when the other prerequisites of capitalist production are present does usury become one of the means assisting in establishing the new mode of production by ruining the feudal lord and small-scale producer, on the one hand, and centralising the conditions of labour into capital on the other.

The Dynamics of Capitalism

In Marx's theory, surplus value is generated by the gap between the value produced by a worker, which is simply the length of the working day, and the value of labour-power. Marx called the part of the working day equivalent to the value of the commodities the worker can buy with the wage, *necessary labour*; the rest is *surplus labour.* Surplus value can be increased by lengthening the working day. This is called *absolute surplus value.* It can also be increased by increasing productivity in the industries producing wage goods (or means of production used in the wage goods industries), thus reducing the value of labour-power (in hours of labour equivalent) without reducing the actual commodities the worker gets. This is *relative surplus value*. Looking at it another way, the surplus product that workers produce can be increased either by making them work for longer (absolute surplus value) or by improving production methods so more is produced in the same time (relative surplus value). Absolute surplus value has a limit, set by physical exhaustion, while relative surplus value does not. Absolute surplus value is important in the early stages of capitalism, and in colonies, where working hours are forced up to the maximum and wages down to the minimum, while relative surplus value dominates in advanced capitalism. Constant efforts to cut costs are forced on capitalists by competition, the primary driving force in capitalism. Any new method of production which reduces costs (a technical improvement, or an 'improvement' in labour discipline) will bring extra profits to those who introduce it quickly, before the general price level has been forced down. Once it is generally adopted, competition forces prices down in line with costs, wiping out any remaining high cost producers. Marx assumed (in general rightly) that large-scale production is more efficient than small-scale. Competition, therefore, forces capitalists to accumulate and reinvest as much as possible in order to produce on a large scale. Marx called growth through reinvestment of profits, *concentration of capital*. Bigger firms will be better able to survive, especially in slumps, and will be able to buy out smaller firms. The growth of the scale of production by amalgamation of capitals is called *centralization of capital.*

Marx described other factors at work in the transition from feudalism to capitalism (while always placing the main stress on the creation of a proletariat): the influx of plunder into England from India and other colonies, the establishment of a world market, the massive growth in mercantile wealth, and so on. The exact role of these external factors is not very clear. The influx of wealth presumably made it easier for prospective capitalists to start businesses and build them up, and it promoted a turnover in the actual personnel of the landowning class, with *nouveau riches* buying out declining and indebted feudal magnates. All this must have acted as a sort of lubricant for the still very slow progress of the capitalist juggernaut. Many recent writers have reversed Marx's emphasis, making the flow of plunder into Europe the main factor in the origins of capitalism (and the failure of capitalist development elsewhere). Marx certainly discussed internal and external factors in primitive accumulation, and the interpretation given above is only one possible reading. I think it accords both with the logic of Marx's case and with the weight of his arguments. A stress on external factors is consistent with a picture of capitalism as a world system divided into centre and periphery, but that was not how Marx saw it. Finally, Marx emphasized the role of the state. Its main function during the process of primitive accumulation (apart from providing legal backing for the expulsion of peasants) was to repress the newly forming working class, and keep their wages down. The organization of the capitalist process of production, once fully developed, breaks down all resistance. The dull compulsion of economic relations completes the subjection of the laborer to the capitalist. Direct force, outside economic conditions, is of course still used, but only exceptionally. It is otherwise during the historical genesis of capitalist production.

Colonialism

Marx did not discuss colonialism in general terms; his views must be deduced from scattered references in his major writings and from articles about special cases, notably about Ireland, about the British empire in India and (much more superficially) about western, particularly British, dealings with China. Marx wrote a considerable amount about Ireland (Marx and Engels 1971), mainly in the form of speeches, passing references in correspondence and the like. He argued that Ireland's poverty and misery, compared with England's status as the leading capitalist centre, were not caused primarily by any internal difference in the prior mode of production, but by external (English) oppression and exploitation. The expulsion of the peasantry and the creation of capitalist farms under the aegis (and to the benefit) of the (English) landed aristocracy followed essentially the same course as in England, though it was carried out with even greater brutality, but: 'every time Ireland was about to develop industrially, she was crushed and reconverted into a purely agricultural land. . . . The people had now before them the choice between occupation of land *at any rent,* or starvation' (Marx and Engels 1971: 132). The main cause of industrial failure in Ireland was the absence of protective tariffs: Irish industry could not survive English competition. In this, Ireland's fate does not seem very different from that of various country districts of England, except for the absence of political constraints on exploitation. Like workers from rural areas of England, the Irish were forced to migrate to seek work in the industrial cities of England. The difference was the existence of a revolutionary (though not socialist) nationalist movement. Marx was especially concerned to see a nationalist revolution against the aristocracy in Ireland, since this would undermine their hold in England, reduce divisions between Irish and English workers in England, and thus advance the socialist revolution inEngland, which 'being the metropolis of capital . is for the present the most important country for the workers revolution, and moreover the *only* country in which the material conditions for this revolution have developed up to a certain degree of maturity' (Marx and Engels 1971: 294). Neither Marx nor Engels thought that revolution in Ireland could be socialist. Engels, after Marx's death, argued that the Irish wanted land, to become independent peasants and 'after that, mortgages will appear on the scene and they will be ruined once more'. They should, however, be encouraged to 'pass from semi-feudal conditions to capitalist conditions' (p. 343). This view of the regressive effect of British rule in Ireland contrasts with Marx's view of its effects in India. The articles about India and China (Marx 1969; Marx and Engels n.d.) were written for the *New York Daily Tribune.* The main series was published during 1853, and includes both commentary on issues of current interest and a number of articles in which Marx set out his considered view on India; these few 'set piece' articles are the main source. In 1853, five years after the writing of the *Communist Manifesto,* Marx had arrived substantially at his mature position, but the economic analysis which culminated in *Capital* was not yet worked out in detail. Where he returned to the same topics in *Capital,* however, there is little sign of any change in his thinking. How much did Marx know about India? It is obvious, both from the articles and from the 'Notes on Indian History' which he compiled, that he had read virtually everything available to him on India and was exceedingly well informed on the political and military history of the sub-continent. There was, however, much that he did not know, probably because no one at that time (or perhaps since) knew it. Thus, in an article of 7 June 1858 (Marx 1969: 313) he discussed debates then going on in England about the real nature of land tenure in India, without firmly coming down in favor of any one interpretation, and in an article of 23 July 1858 (Marx 1969: 330) he discussed contemporary debates about the burden of taxation in India without being able to settle the question of whether or not Indian cultivators are 'overtaxed', in the sense that taxation threatens the resources needed for reproduction. These two issues (land tenure or the relations of production, and the extent of exploitation and the size of the potential surplus product) should presumably be crucial to a Marxist analysis of Indian society, but the information was simply not available.

Marx examined the origins and development of the East India Company, arguing that it had from an early date two objects: to develop trade, and also to 'make territorial revenue one of sources of emolument'. As the company's territories expanded from the middle of the eighteenth century to the middle of the nineteenth, the time when Marx was writing, it came more and more under the control of the British state, creating a peculiar hybrid of public and private power typical of the oligarchic British state of that epoch. The whole character of the British relationship with India was transformed in the early nineteenth century by the rise of industrial capital. Before then, Indian textiles were among products exported to Britain, with a drain of precious metals to India to pay for them.

Labour Aristocracy

Based on imperialism, Lenin and Bukharin were grappling with the most immediate political problems of their time. With the outbreak of the First World War, the majority of workers in the main belligerent countries had supported the war effort of their own states. The working classes of Europe were, at that very moment, killing each other on the battlefields. This horrifying fact ran completely counter to Marx's prediction: The working men have no country. National differences and antagonisms between peoples are daily more and more vanishing owing to the development of the bourgeoisie, to freedom of commerce, to the world market, to uniformity in the mode of production and in the conditions of life corresponding thereto. The theory of imperialism explained why there should be antagonism between the ruling classes of different countries, the beneficiaries of the 'state capitalist trusts' or 'monopoly capitalist combines'. It remained to explain how the proletariat could be infected by aggressive nationalism. Hilferding, writing before the war, saw imperialism as directly opposed to the interests of the working class, even in the dominant countries. He argued that the close links between the state and capital reveal the class character of the state, and lead the proletariat to adopt a stance of opposition to the state and to imperialism. This over-optimistic estimate could not be sustained when Bukharin and Lenin were writing. They argued that sections of the working class in the dominant countries did benefit from the monopoly position their capitalist masters had in the world market, and that this explains the support that the imperialist powers were able to gain from the working-class movement. They also argued (though not in detail) that this gain only accrued to some workers, and that it was merely a relative gain: workers employed by a monopoly in an advanced country did better than those in a weaker position, but all would do better in a socialist society. The main argument that Lenin, in particular, relied on, however, was that imperialism made war inevitable, and that the horrors of war totally wiped out any gains the workers might get from monopolistic privilege. Bukharin set the context like this: The first period of the war has brought about, not a crisis of capitalism . But a collapse of the 'Socialist' International. This phenomenon, which many have attempted to explain by proceeding solely from the analysis of the internal relations in every country, cannot be more or less satisfactorily explained from this angle. For the collapse of the proletarian movement is a result of the unequal situation of the 'state capitalist trusts' within the boundaries of world economy. (*IWE*: 161) His argument was fairly straightforward. There is always a tendency in capitalist economies for workers to identify with their employers, on the basis that: 'the better the business of our shop, the better for me'. The evolution of trades union struggle has largely wiped out this attachment to a particular enterprise or industry and replaced it with an awareness of the need to unite against the capitalist employers. At the same time, however, the formation of 'state capitalist trusts' has created a basis for solidarity between classes on the national level, the 'so called working class protectionism with its policy of safeguarding "national industry", "national labour", etc.' (*IWE*: 162-3). The competitive struggle has been transformed into a struggle in the world market between state monopoly trusts. The stronger trusts gain monopoly profit. They also gain extra profit by exploiting native labour in the colonies. These extra profits are the basis for the payment of increased wages. The workers in the dominant countries therefore gain from the success of 'their' states in the competitive struggle.

Lenin's arguments follow the same lines, but are rather broader and less specific (on Lenin's version, Szymanski 1981, ch. 14). He was more insistent that it is only a section of the workers who gain, and he also emphasized the possession of colonies more strongly, quoting Engels, who had discussed the reactionary political stance of the English working class as early as 1858. The significance of this, though Lenin did not bring it out, is that Engels (and Lenin) described the emergence of a 'labour aristocracy' *before* the rise of monopoly (in the sense of control of a market by a single enterprise or organized group of enterprises). This seems inconsistent with Lenin's own comment 'the economic possibility of such bribery, whatever its form may be, requires high monopolist profits' (*Imperialism*: 540). Let us first consider the case of an enterprise which gains high profits because of its monopoly control of markets. It is clearly possible for such a firm to pay higher wages to its workers than it could without a protected monopoly position. There is, nothing in its monopoly position that compels it to pay higher wages. If workers are effectively organized in trades unions, they can try to insist on higher wages, and the sheltered economic position of the employers may reduce their resistance to this pressure. Alternatively, a firm may decide to pay higher wages in order to forestall trades unionism, or to gain the loyalty of its workers. The gains are very likely, in this case, to go to a privileged minority, if the management chooses to 'divide and rule'. Workers' gains may be in terms of better working conditions, shorter hours or better conditions of work, rather than in higher wages. Against this must be set the possibility, emphasized by Hilferding, that a larger firm with greater financial resources may be in a stronger position to resist wage claims and to suppress trades unions, especially if it can call on state support in these conflicts. The stronger economic position of large monopoly firms may thus lead to better or worse conditions for workers, depending on the precise balance of forces. Lenin, in particular, seems to suggest a conscious policy of the ruling class in his repeated use of the word 'bribe' to describe the gains of the workers. All the classical Marxists tended to overstate the extent to which monopoly had triumphed. In fact, it was still the exception, rather than the rule, for a single firm or organized cartel to have complete control over the market for a product, even within the protected boundaries of a single advanced country, and in the world market as a whole, price competition was very far from being suppressed. This difficulty is compounded by Lenin's insistence on tracing the history of the 'labour aristocracy' back to nineteenth century England, when there certainly were many competing firms. We must look at the case where a particular country has a monopoly position in the production of some commodity, either in the world market or in colonial markets, but where there are many small firms competing with each other within the country concerned. The main point is that no single firm can afford to concede higher wages unless its competitors do the same. The fact that the firms in the industry have a monopoly as a group makes little difference when there is competition within the group. The only way workers can gain is by a general wage increase across the whole industry, and this can only be achieved by some force that operates at that level. A general shortage of labour in the industry is one such factor (which might be the product of its success in gaining control of markets), a strong trades union organization is another, and the intervention of the state is a third.

Both Bukharin and Lenin have correctly identified skilled workers as the better-off stratum of the working class, and therefore tended to identify them as the beneficiaries of imperialism. In fact, differentials between skilled and unskilled workers were of great antiquity, and it is not clear that skilled workers, as a group, did particularly well out of imperialism. To analyse the point further would require an analysis of the world division of labour. One could argue that the work done by unskilled workers is more easily transferred to establishments in colonies where cheap labour can be employed, and that skilled workers are more protected from this kind of competition. It should also be pointed out that capital export works counter to the workers' interests, at least in the longer run, by creating jobs abroad at the expense of jobs at home, although it may, in the short run, encourage the production of capital goods for export and thus keep up employment in the industries concerned.

Bukharin and Lenin observed that the living standards of some workers in some advanced countries had risen significantly, and that they no longer had 'nothing to lose but their chains'. At the same time, the countries where this was happening were also those which were coming out on top in the struggle for world dominance. Our authors deserve great credit for recognizing that a 'national interest' does exist, at least to a certain degree, and that sectional and nationalistic sentiments among the working class have a real material basis. There can be no doubt that stratification of the working class is a very important issue, but subsequent writers have not generally sought to explain it in terms of colonial profits or in terms of monopoly in world markets. Kautsky argued that this policy of 'peaceful' joint exploitation of the world by the united finance capital of the great powers would be forced on them by the threat they faced from the oppressed colonial peoples and from their own proletariat. It is clear, incidentally, that in describing ultra-imperialism as 'peaceful', Kautsky did not mean that exploited peoples or the proletariat at the centre would be treated with kid gloves. He simply meant that the ruling classes of the major capitalist powers would not go to war with each other. The way this theory was posed, and the way it was attacked by the left, reveal a great deal about the concepts of imperialism shared by both sides in the debate. Kautsky argued that the stress might shift from conflict between imperialist powers to maintenance of a world system of exploitation. It is surely the latter, the world-wide suppression of colonial peoples by the metropolitan bourgeoisie, which is generally understood by the term 'imperialism' today, but Kautsky was careful to distinguish it from imperialism as the term was then understood, and to give it a different name. The very suggestion that such a shift was possible aroused vehement hostility from the left.

Secondly, this tendency in fact dominant at the time of the First World War, or, alternatively, was it reasonable to expect it to become dominant within a fairly short time? Third, does this theory have anything to offer in understanding the world today? There is no space here to deal fully with the second of these questions, since detailed historical and empirical material would be required. Those who criticized Kautsky at the time could, of course, only consider the first two of these questions. The central reason for left-wing opposition to the theory of ultra imperialism is obvious. Lenin and his allies thought that a socialist revolution was on the cards for the near future, and they wanted to argue that war and misery were the only alternative to revolution. In the context of the First World War, idle dreams of the possibility of lasting peace after the war were a diversion from the real issues. Both Bukharin and, especially, Lenin wrote about imperialism primarily to challenge Kautsky's view, and to repair the damage done to the international socialist movement by the capitulation of the parties of the Second International at the outbreak of the war. As far as they were concerned, the intimate connection between capitalist development, imperialism, and war was the central theoretical basis of their stand against abandoning the struggle for socialism for the duration. No compromise on this issue was possible. Lenin has vehemently rejected any idea of ultra-imperialism: 'development is proceeding towards monopolies, hence towards a single world monopoly as completely meaningless as is the statement that "development is proceeding" towards the manufacture of foodstuffs in laboratories' (*Imperialism*: 530). Bukharin was more moderate: in the abstract a world trust is thinkable, but in reality it cannot come about. He advanced two reasons for this. First, any agreement between 'state capitalist trusts' must be disrupted by uneven development. The strong will not in any case accept agreements since they will hope to gain moreIf the proletariat became strong enough to prevent aggressive policies, as Kautsky hoped they might, they would be strong enough to establish socialism. Hilferding, who wrote before Kautsky's theory of ultra-imperialism was devised, put the same argument, but did not come to any conclusion as to whether force or peaceful division of the market would prevail, though he thought that agreements were only likely to be temporary. The first of Bukharin's arguments rests on the assumption that national blocs of capital, each exploiting exclusive possession of a national economic territory, must remain the basic units between which any ultra-imperialist peace would be made. However, in addition to the reasons Bukharin put forward for the formation of nationally based 'state capitalist trusts', there is a counter-tendency, also arising from factors included in his analysis.

Bukharin, as for Hilferding, an important motive for capital export is the desire to penetrate the protected markets of other nation states from within local place. Over a long period of time, this can lead to interpenetration of national capitals, with the same group of firms operating within each national economic territory. In this case, a struggle to enlarge one nation's territory at the expense of others becomes economically pointless. To give an example, there would be no point in Ford or General Motors seeking to extend their markets by sponsoring US annexation of parts of the EEC, when they are securely established in the European industry already. In the same way, tariff barriers between different markets become a hindrance rather than a benefit once multinational firms are well established. As for the second argument, that if the working class is strong enough to compel the adoption of peaceful policies it will also be strong enough to overthrow capitalism, this seems an extremely schematic argument which does not do adequate justice to the complexity of political developments. All of our authors anticipated socialist revolutions in the advanced countries within a fairly short period of time. We have, in fact, seen the emergence of a socialist bloc, and of Third World liberation movements which pose a massive threat to world capitalism, forcing the major capitalist states onto the defensive, together with a political absorption of the working class into a reshaped political system. It is clear that the orthodox objections to the theory of ultra-imperialism no longer have the same force.

CHAPTER - IV

CRITICISM ON LABOR MOVEMENT BY WRITERS, POETS

Labor Criticism by Writers

France declared war on Austria, and rumors that the king was guilty of treason turned the people against him. In 1792 a second revolution created the Commune of Paris, which suspended the power of the king and prompted arrests of suspected royalists. The September Massacres occurred thereafter, when mobs murdered 2,000 of these prisoners. The Republic was declared in 1792, and it became increasingly radicalized until Maximilien Robespierre took control and instituted the Reign of Terror, in which many were guillotined including the king and queen. The Revolution drew to a close with the death by guillotine of Robespierre himself in 1794 and the rise to power of Napoleon.

Eliot was explicit about the mythical aspect of her novel. She told John Blackwood, her publisher, that 'It came to me first of all, quite suddenly, as a sort of legendary tale, suggested by my recollection of having once, in early childhood, seen a linen weaver with a bag on his back; but as my mind dwelt on the subject, I became inclined to a more realistic treatment.' She still gave her narrative some of the properties of a fairy story: the drawing of lots to decide a man's fate, the miser with his bags of gold, the foundling child. After being unjustly cast out by his religious community in the town where he plies his trade, Silas Marner arrives at Raveloe as a mysterious outsider, and for the first half of the novel remains so. While the villagers pay him to weave linen for them, he becomes a figure of superstition, feared by the local children. He lives in solitude just outside the village, accumulating gold for his labours, growing 'withered and yellow' by the narrowness of his occupation.

'The Weaver of Raveloe', draws attention to the influence of labour as well as Silas's legendary status. Eliot was often interested in the work undertaken by the principal figures in her novels, and unusual amongst Victorian novelists in making many of these skilled labourers: Adam Bede is a carpenter, Felix Holt a watchmaker. Labour has formed many of the characters. In the scene in which Godfrey and Nancy visit Silas to offer to adopt Eppie, Eliot feels for the smallest sign of this influence. As Nancy assures her that she will want for nothing as the daughter of the squire and his wife, she grasps Marner's hand firmly, noticing what we notice: 'it was a weaver's hand, with a palm and finger-tips that were sensitive to such pressure'. The detail, both psychologically and physiologically exact, is characteristic of Eliot.

In the early parts of the novel, Godfrey Cass and his feckless younger brother Dunstan are unusual in apparently having no work to do. Their idleness condemns them to vice and folly. In pre-Victorian English fiction there was no obvious stigma attached to being without employment. A 'gentleman' was usually, indeed, someone who did not have to work for a living. By contrast, few Victorian novels are without instances of the ennobling influence of work. One of the bestsellers of Eliot's age, Samuel Smiles's *Self-Help* is a celebration of 'industry' as a personal virtue and of 'energetic' labourers of every class. For Smiles, indolence is the ultimate vice. Godfrey and Dunstan's father has an estate to run, and almost everyone else in the village is defined by their occupation. Even Godfrey's bride to be, the lovely Nancy, a farmer's daughter, makes cheese and butter with her own hands. Near the end of the novel, Silas takes Eppie back to the town where he had once lived and finds, in place of Lantern Yard, 'a large factory, from which men and women were streaming for their mid-day meal' (ch. 21). This is the coming world, where labour is no longer individualistic and men and women are but particles in a stream.

Literature & Poets

American poetry: the poetry of the United States, arose first as efforts by colonists to add their voices to English poetry in the 17th century, well before the constitutional unification of the thirteen colonies (although before this unification, a strong oral tradition often likened to poetry existed among Native American societies). Unsurprisingly, most of the early colonists' work relied on contemporary British models of poetic form, diction, and theme. However, in the 19th century, a distinctive American idiom began to emerge. By the later part of that century, when Walt Whitman was winning an enthusiastic audience abroad, poets from the United States had begun to take their place at the forefront of the English-language *avant-garde.*

The history of American poetry is not easy to know. Much of the American poetry published between 1910 and 1945 remains lost in the pages of small circulation political periodicals, particularly the ones on the far left, destroyed by librarians during the 1950s McCarthy era. The received narrative of Modernism proposes that Ezra Pound and T. S. Eliot were perhaps the most influential modernist English-language poets in the period during World War I. But this narrative leaves out African American and women poets who were published and read widely in the first half of the twentieth century. By the 1960s, the young poets of the British Poetry Revival looked to their American contemporaries and predecessors as models for the kind of poetry they wanted to write. Toward the end of the millennium, consideration of

American poetry had diversified, as scholars placed an increased emphasis on poetry by women, African Americans, Hispanics, Chicanos and other cultural groupings.

Poetry in the Colonies

As England's contact with the Americas increased after the 1490s, explorers sometimes included verse with their descriptions of the "New World" up through 1650, the year of Anne Bradstreet's "The Tenth Muse", which was written in America, most likely in Ipswich, Massachusetts or North Andover, Massachusetts) and printed/distributed in London, England by her brother-in-law, Rev. John Woodbridge. There are 14 such writers whom we might on that basis call American poets (they had actually been to America and to different degrees, written poems or verses about the place). Early examples include a 1616 "testimonial poem" on the sterling warlike character of Captain John Smith (in Barbour, ed. "Works") and Rev. William Morrell's 1625 "Nova Anglia" or "New England," which is a rhymed catalog of everything from American weather to glimpses of Native women, framed with a thin poetic "conceit" or "fiction" characterizing the country as a "sad and forlorn" female pining for English domination. Then in May 1627 Thomas Morton of Merry mount, an English West Country outdoorsman, attorney at law, man of letters and colonial adventurer, raised a Maypole to celebrate and foster more success at this fur-trading plantation and nailed up a "Poem" and "Song" (one a densely literary manifesto on how English and Native people came together there and must keep doing so for a successful America; the other a light "drinking song" also full of deeper American implications). These were published in book form along with other examples of Morton's American poetry in "New English Canaan" (1637); and based on the criteria of "First," "American" and Poetry," they make Morton (and not Anne Bradstreet) America's first poet in English.

One of the first recorded poets of the British colonies was Anne Bradstreet (1612 – 1672), who remains one of the earliest known women poets who wrote in English. The poems she published during her lifetime address religious and political themes. She also wrote tender evocations of home, family life and of her love for her husband, many of which remained unpublished until the 20th century.

Edward Taylor (1645–1729) wrote poems expounding Puritan virtues in a highly wrought metaphysical style that can be seen as typical of the early colonial period.

This narrow focus on the Puritan ethic was, understandably, the dominant note of most of the poetry written in the colonies during the 17th and early 18th centuries. The earliest "secular" poetry published in New England was by Samuel Danforth in his "almanacks" for

1647–1649, published at Cambridge; these included "puzzle poems" as well as poems on caterpillars, pigeons, earthquakes, and hurricanes. Of course, being a Puritan minister as well as a poet, Danforth never ventured far from a spiritual message. A distinctly American lyric voice of the colonial period was Phillis Wheatley, a slave whose book "Poems on Various Subjects, Religious and Moral," was published in 1773. She was one of the best-known poets of her day, at least in the colonies, and her poems were typical of New England culture at the time, meditating on religious and classical ideas.

The 18th century saw an increasing emphasis on America itself as fit subject matter for its poets. This trend is most evident in the works of Philip Freneau (1752–1832), who is also notable for the unusually sympathetic attitude to Native Americans shown in his writings, sometimes reflective of a skepticism toward Anglo-American culture and civilization. However, as might be expected from what was essentially provincial writing, this late colonial poetry is generally somewhat old-fashioned in form and syntax, deploying the means and methods of Pope and Gray in the era of Blake and Burns. The work of Rebecca Hammond Lard (1772–1855), although quite old, still apply to life in today's world. She writes about nature, not only the nature of environment, but also the nature of humans. On the whole, the development of poetry in the American colonies mirrors the development of the colonies themselves. The early poetry is dominated by the need to preserve the integrity of the Puritan ideals that created the settlement in the first place. As the colonists grew in confidence, the poetry they wrote increasingly reflected their drive towards independence. This shift in subject matter was not reflected in the mode of writing which tended to be conservative, to say the least. This can be seen as a product of the physical remove at which American poets operated from the center of English-language poetic developments in London.

Whitman and Dickinson

The final emergence of a truly indigenous English-language poetry in the United States was the work of two poets, Walt Whitman (1819–1892) and Emily Dickinson (1830–1886). On the surface, these two poets could not have been less alike. Whitman's long lines, derived from the metric of the King James Version of the Bible, and his democratic inclusiveness stand in stark contrast with Dickinson's concentrated phrases and short lines and stanzas, derived from Protestant hymnals.

Modernism and After

The combined with a study of 19th-century French poetry, formed the basis of American input into 20th-century English-language poetic modernism. Ezra Pound (1885–1972) and

T. S. Eliot (1888–1965) were the leading figures at the time, with their rejection of traditional poetic form and meter and of Victorian diction. Both steered American poetry toward greater density, difficulty, and opacity, with an emphasis on techniques such as fragmentation, ellipsis, allusion, juxtaposition, ironic and shifting personae, and mythic parallelism. Pound, in particular, opened up American poetry to diverse influences, including the traditional poetries of China and Japan.

T.S. Eliot

Numerous other poets made important contributions at this revolutionary juncture, including Gertrude Stein (1874–1946), Wallace Stevens (1879–1955), William Carlos Williams (1883–1963), Hilda Doolittle (H.D.) (1886–1961), Marianne Moore (1887–1972), E.E. Cummings (1894–1962), and Hart Crane (1899–1932). The cerebral and skeptical Romantic Stevens helped revive the philosophical lyric, and Williams was to become exemplary for many later poets because he, more than any of his peers, contrived to marry spoken American English with free verse rhythms. Cummings remains notable for his experiments with typography and evocation of a spontaneous vision of reality.

Whereas these poets were unambiguously aligned with high modernism, other poets active in the United States in the first third of the 20th century were not. Among the most important of the latter were those who were associated with what came to be known as the New Criticism. These included John Crowe Ransom (1888–1974), Allen Tate (1899–1979), and Robert Penn Warren (1905–1989). Other poets of the era, such as Archibald MacLeish (1892–1982), experimented with modernist techniques but were also drawn towards more traditional modes of writing. Still others, such as Robinson Jeffers (1887–1962), adopted Modernist freedom while remaining aloof from Modernist factions and programs. In addition, there were still other, early 20th Century poets who maintained or were forced to maintain a peripheral relationship to high modernism, likely due to the racially charged themes of their work. They include Countee Cullen (1903–1946), *Alice Dunbar Nelson (1875–1935),* Gwendolyn Bennett (1902–1981), Langston Hughes (1902–1967), *Claude McKay (1889–1948),* Jean Toomer (1894–1967) and other African American poets of the Harlem Renaissance.

The modernist torch was carried in the 1930s mainly by the group of poets known as the Objectivists. These included Louis Zukofsky (1904–1978), Charles Reznikoff (1894–1976), George Oppen (1908–1984), Carl Rakosi (1903–2004) and, later, Lorine Niedecker (1903–1970). Kenneth Rexroth, who was published in the *Objectivist Anthology*, was, along with

Madeline Gleason (1909–1973), a forerunner of the San Francisco Renaissance. Many of the Objectivists came from **urban communities of new immigrants**, and this new vein of experience and language enriched the growing American idiom.

Elizabeth Barrett Browning: Social and Political Issues

Themes: *Victorian poetry, Power and politics*

From industrialization to slavery, **Dr Simon Avery** looks at the 19th century social and political issues that fed into Elizabeth Barrett Browning's poetry. ***Elizabeth Barrett Browning (1806-1861) was one of the most famous and prolific poets of the Victorian period***, with a career spanning four decades. During this time she established herself as a woman who was never afraid to express her views on contemporary social and political issues, a position which often marked her out as unconventional and combative. While more conservative women poets wrote about nature, pious religion or the domestic space, Elizabeth Barrett Browning wrote about industrialization, slavery, political leadership, religious controversy, the problems faced by women in society, and what it was like to live in the modern world. She always questioned and judged conventional views.

Rise of Conservatism within the Second Republic

Naturally, the provisional government was disorganized as it attempted to deal with France's economic problems. The conservative elements of French society were wasting no time in organizing against the provisional government. After roughly a month, conservatives began to openly oppose the new government, using the rallying cry "order", which the new republic lacked.

Additionally, there was a major split between the citizens of Paris and those citizens of the more rural areas of France. The provisional government set out to establish deeper government control of the economy and guarantee a more equal distribution of resources. As noted above, to deal with the unemployment problem, the provisional government established National Workshops. The unemployed were given jobs building roads and planting trees without regard for the demand for these tasks. The population of Paris ballooned as job seekers from all over France came to Paris to work in the newly formed National Workshops. To pay for these the new National Workshops and the other social programs, the provisional government placed new taxes on land. These taxes alienated the "landed classes" especially the small farmers and the peasantry of the rural areas of France from the provisional government. Hardworking rural farmers were resistant to paying for the unemployed city people and their new "Right to Work" National Workshops. The taxes were widely disobeyed in the rural areas and, thus, the government remained strapped for cash. Popular uncertainty about the liberal foundations of the provisional government became apparent in the 23 April 1848 elections. Despite, the agitation from the left, voters elected a constituent assembly which was primarily moderate and conservative. In May, Jacques-Charles Dupont de l'Eure, chairman of the provisional government, made way for the Executive Commission, a body of state acting as Head of State with five co-presidents.

The results of the 23 April 1848 election were a disappointment to the radicals in Paris except for the election of one candidate popular among urban workers, François-Vincent Raspail. Many radicals felt the elections were a sign of the slowing down of the revolutionary movement. These radicals in Paris pressured the government to head an international "crusade" for democracy. Independence of other European states, such as Poland was urged by the Paris radicals. In 1848, Poland as a national state, did not exist. The nation of Poland had been gradually "partitioned" or divided between foreign powers of Prussia, Russia, and Austria in 1773, 1793.Finally in 1795, all of the Polish nation was swallowed up by the three powers. However, it was an opportune time to raise the issue of Polish independence as Poles were also undergoing their own period of revolt in 1848 starting with the uprising in Poznań on 20 March 1848. (Wielkopolska Uprising.)

However, the government of the National Constituent Assembly continued to resist the radicals. The radicals began to protest against the National Constituent Assembly government. On 15 May 1848, Parisian workmen feeling their democratic and social republic was slipping away, invaded the Assembly *en masse* and proclaimed a new Provisional Government. This attempted revolution on the part of the working classes was quickly suppressed by the National Guard. The leaders of this revolt Louis Auguste Blanqui, Armand Barbès, François Vincent Raspail and others were arrested. The trial of these leaders was held in Bourges, France, from March 7 to April 3, 1849.

The conservative classes of society were becoming increasingly fearful of the power of the working classes in Paris. They felt a strong need for organization and organized themselves around the need for "order" the so-called "Party of Order." For the Party of Order the term "order" meant a roll back of society to days of Louis Philippe. The Party of Order was now the dominant member of the government. As the main force of reaction against revolution, the Party of Order forced the closure of the hated Right to Work National Workshops on 21 June 1848. On 23 June 1848, the working class of Paris rose in protest over the closure of the National Workshops. On that day 170,000 citizens of Paris came out into the streets to erect barricades. To meet this challenge, the government appointed General Louis Eugène Cavaignac to lead the military forces suppressing the uprising of the working classes. General Cavaignac had been serving in the Army in Algeria. Cavaignac had returned from Algeria and in the elections of 23 April 1848, he was elected to the National Constituent Assembly. Cavaignac arrived in Paris only on 17 May 1848 to take his seat in the National Assembly.

Barricades on rue Saint-Maur during the uprising Between 23 June and 26 June 1848, this battle between the working class and Cavaignac came to be known as the June Days Uprising. Cavaignac's forces started out on 23 June 1848 with an army composed of from 20,000 to 30,000 soldiers of the Paris garrison of the French Army. Cavaignac began a systematic assault against the revolutionary Parisian citizenry, targeting the blockaded areas of the city. However, he was not able to break the stiff opposition put up by the armed workers on the barricades on 23 June 1848. Accordingly, Cavaignac's forces were reinforced with another 20,000–25,000 soldiers from the mobile guard, some additional 60,000 to 80,000 from the national guard. Even with this force of 120,000 to 125,000 soldiers, Cavaignac still required two days to complete the suppression of the working-class uprising.

In February 1848, the workers and *petite bourgeoisie* had fought together, but now, in June 1848, the lines were drawn differently. The working classes had been abandoned by the bourgeois politicians who founded the provisional government. This would prove fatal to the Second Republic, which, without the support of the working classes, could not continue. Although the governmental regime of the Second Republic continued to survive until December 1852, the generous, idealistic Republic to which the February Days had given birth, ended with the suppression of the "June Days."

The "Party of Order" moved quickly to consolidate the forces of reaction in the government and on 28 June 1848, the government appointed Louis Eugène Cavaignac as the head of the French state. On 10 December 1848 a presidential election was held between four candidates. Cavaignac, was the candidate of the Party of Order. Alexandre Auguste Ledru-Rollin was also a candidate in that presidential election. Ledru-Rollin was the editor of the *La Réforme* newspaper and as such was the leader of the radical democrats among the petty bourgeoisie. François-Vincent Raspail was the candidate of the revolutionary working classes. Louis-Napoléon Bonaparte was the fourth presidential candidate. Napoleon III won the presidential election of 10 December 1848 with 5,587,759 votes as opposed to 1,474,687 votes for Cavaignac and 370,000 votes for Ledru-Rollin. Raspail ended up a distant fourth in the balloting.

Class Struggles within the Revolution

Karl Marx saw the "June Days" uprising as strong evidence of class conflict. Marx saw the 1848 Revolution as being directed by the desires of the middle-class. While the bourgeoisie agitated for "proper participation", workers had other concerns. Many of the participants in the revolution were of the so-called *petite bourgeoisie* (small business owners). In 1848, the "petite" or petty bourgeoisie outnumbered the working classes (unskilled laborers in mines, factories and stores, paid to perform manual labor and other work rather than for their expertise) by about two to one. However, the petty bourgeoisie was greatly indebted due to the economic recession of 1846–1847. By 1848, overdue business debt was 21,000,000 francs in Paris and 11,000,000 francs in the provinces. The February Revolution united all classes against Louis Philippe. The bourgeoisie joined with the working classes to fight for "proper participation" in the government for all sections and classes in society. But after the revolution, the working classes were disillusioned by their small share of that participation, and revolted in the streets. This frightened the bourgeoisie and they repressed the uprising during the June Days. The petit bourgeoisie worked the hardest to suppress the revolt. Its financial condition had deteriorated even further due to slow sales and economic dislocations of the Revolution. As of June 1848, over 7,000 shopkeepers and merchants in Paris had not paid their rent since February. During the June Days, their creditors and landlords (the finance bourgeoisie), forestalled most attempts to collect on those debts. But once the worker revolt was put down, they began to assert their claims in court. Thus, the financial bourgeoisie turned their back on the petty bourgeoisie. Bankruptcies and foreclosures rose dramatically. The petty bourgeoisie staged a large demonstration at the National Assembly to demand that the government inquire into the problem of foreclosures and for debt to be extended for businessmen who could prove that their insolvency was caused by the Revolution. Such a plan was introduced in the National Assembly but was rejected. The petty bourgeoisie was pauperized and many small merchants became part of the working class.

Accordingly, the provisional government, supposedly created to address the concerns of all the classes of French society, had little support among the working classes and petit bourgeoisie. Therefore, it tended to address only the concerns of the liberal bourgeoisie. Support for the provisional government was especially weak in the countryside, which was predominantly agricultural and more conservative, and had its own concerns, such as food shortages due to bad harvests. The concerns of the bourgeoisie were very different from those of the lower classes. Support for the provisional government was also undermined by the memory of the French Revolution.

The "Thermidorian reaction" and the ascent of Napoleon III to the throne are evidence that the people preferred the safety of an able dictatorship to the uncertainty of revolution. Louis Napoleon portrayed himself as "rising above politics". Each class in France saw Louis Napoleon as a return of the "great days" of Napoleon Bonaparte, but had its own vision of such a return. Karl Marx was referring to this phenomenon when he said "History repeats itself ;the first time as a tragedy, the second time as a farce." Thus, the various classes and political groupings had different reasons for supporting Napoleon in the election of December 10, 1848. Napoleon himself encouraged this by "being all things to all people". Legitimists (Bourbons) and Orleans (Citizen King Louis-Philippe) monarchists saw Louis Napoleon as the beginning of a royalist restoration in France. The army believed Napoleon would have a foreign policy of war. The industrial bourgeoisie felt that Napoleon would suppress further revolutionary activity. The petty bourgeoisie saw Napoleon as the rule of the debtor over the creditor, and as their savior against the large finance capitalists. Even some of the proletariat supported Louis Napoleon (over the petty bourgeoisie socialist Alexandre Ledru-Rollin) in order to remove the hated Cavaignac and the bourgeoisie republicanism of the National Assembly which had betrayed the proletarian interests in the recent June Days.

Peasants overwhelmingly supported Napoleon. Thus, one might argue, without the support of these large lower classes, the revolution of 1848 would not carry through, despite the hopes of the liberal bourgeoisie.

End of the Revolution in France

Following the repression of the June Days, the French Revolution of 1848 was basically over. Politics in France continued to tilt to the right, as the era of revolution in France came to an end. However the Party of Order and the Cavaignac dictatorship were still fearful of another popular uprising in the streets. Accordingly, on 2 September 1848, the government continued the state of siege that had been in place since the June Days. Also on 2 September 1848, the National Constituent Assembly vowed not to dissolve itself until they had written a new constitution and enacted all the organic laws necessary to implement that new constitution. Although the National Constituent Assembly had attempted to write a constitution before the June Days, only a "first draft" of that constitution had been written before the repression in June 1848.This first draft, however, still contained the phrase "Right to Work" and contained several provisions dealing with the demands of the working classes. In the eyes of the Party of Order, these provisions were now entirely unacceptable, especially in the new conservative political environment after the June Days. Accordingly, on 4 September 1848, the National

Constituent Assembly, now controlled by the Party of Order, set about writing a new constitution. "The new constitution was finished on 23 October 1848 and presidential elections were scheduled for 10 December 1848. As noted above Louis Napoleon won the presidential election by a wide margin over the current dictator Louis Cavaignac and the petty bourgeoisie socialist Alexandre Ledru-Rollin. Louis Napoleon's family name of *Napoleon* rallied support to his cause. Elected with Louis Napoleon was a National Assembly which was filled with monarchists of either the Legitimist (Bourbon) variety or the Orleanist (Louis-Philippe) variety. As noted above the Bourbons tended to support the landed aristocracy while the Orleanist tended to support the banking and finance bourgeoisie. One of those elected to the National Assembly was Adolphe Thiers who was the leader of the Orleanist party. As such, Thiers became the chief spokesman of the finance bourgeoisie, however as time went by he was tending to speak for the whole bourgeoisie, including the rising industrial bourgeoisie. After sweeping the elections, Louis Napoleon tried to return France to the old order. Although, Napoleon purged republicans and returned the "vile multitude" (including Adolphe Thiers) to its former place, Napoleon III was unable to totally turn the clock back. Indeed, the presidency of Louis Napoleon, followed by the Second Empire, would be a time of great industrialization and great economic expansion of railroads and banking. By the time of the December 2, 1851 coup, Louis Napoleon had dissolved the National Assembly without having the constitutional right to do so, and became the sole ruler of France. Cells of resistance surfaced, but were put down, and the Second Republic was officially over. He re-established universal suffrage, feared by the Republicans at the time who correctly expected the countryside to vote against the Republic, Louis Napoleon took the title Emperor Napoleon III, and the Second Empire began.

Charles Dickens : Social Commentator and Critic

Dickens was not only the first great urban novelist in England, but also one of the most important social commentators who used fiction effectively to criticize economic, social, and moral abuses in the Victorian era. Dickens showed compassion and empathy towards the vulnerable and disadvantaged segments of English society, and contributed to several important social reforms. Dickens's deep social commitment and awareness of social ills are derived from his traumatic childhood experiences when his father was imprisoned in the Marshal sea Debtors' Prison under the Insolvent Debtors Act of 1813, and he at the age of twelve worked in a shoe-blacking factory. In his adult life Dickens developed a strong social conscience, an ability to empathize with the victims of social and economic injustices. In a letter to his friend Wilkie Collins dated September 6, 1858, Dickens writes of the importance of social commitment: "Everything that happens, shows beyond mistake that you can't shut out the world; that you are in it, to be of it; that you get yourself into a false position the moment you try to sever yourself from it; that you must mingle with it, and make the best of it, and make the best of yourself into the bargain" (Marlow, 132).

Dickens believed in the ethical and political potential of literature, and the novel in particular, and he treated his fiction as a springboard for debates about moral and social reform. In his novels of social analysis Dickens became an outspoken critic of unjust economic and social conditions. His deeply-felt social commentaries helped raise the collective awareness of the reading public. Dickens contributed significantly to the emergence of public opinion which was gaining an increasing influence on the decisions of the authorities. Indirectly, *he contributed to a series of legal reforms, including the abolition of the inhumane imprisonment for debts, purification of the Magistrates' courts, a better management of criminal prisons, and the restriction of the capital punishment.*

The Novel a Repository of Social Conscience

Dickens was a great moralist and a perceptive social commentator. He was by no means completely under the influence of Carlyle, but he followed his teaching when he exposed the ills of Victorian society. Although his fiction was not politically subversive, he called to remedy acute social abuses. After Dickens's death his social theory was long regarded as oversimplified, but as Jane Smiley pointed out in *The Guardian*, in recent years it has been reassessed:

> For example, in the 1960s and 70s, the era of the new left, Dickens was considered well-meaning but naive; his "programme" was thought to be poorly worked out and inconsistent-not Marxist enough (though Marx was a great fan of Dickens). After Marxism went out of fashion, Dickens's amorphous social critique came to seem more universally true because it was not programmatic but based on feelings of generosity and brotherhood combined with specific criticisms of practices common in England during his lifetime. [June 24, 2006]

Dickens was not the first novelist to draw attention of the reading public to the deprivation of the lower classes in England, but he was much more successful than his predecessors in exposing the ills of the industrial society including class division, poverty, bad sanitation, privilege and meritocracy and the experience of the metropolis. In common with many nineteenth-century authors, Dickens used the novel as a repository of social conscience. However, as Louis James argues:

Dickens is at once central and untypical in the 'social novel'. A novelist universally associated with social issues, he was attacked for allowing his imagination to come between his writing and his subject, and his underlying attitudes can be evasive. In his fiction, most characters have a job; but Dickens rarely shows them at work. His novels are centrally about social relationships, yet his model for this would seem, as Cazamian noted, a perpetual Christmas of warm feelings, and the benevolent paternalism of Fezziwig in *A Christmas Carol* (1843). Even his explicit working-out of class and industrial issues in *Hard Times* (1854), based on a hasty visit to a factory strike in Preston, identified the factory problem not with economics but with the Utilitarian denial of human imagination, and juxtaposed the factories of Coketown against the bizarre world of Sleary's travelling circus. [548]

However much radicals admired him, Dickens was never a radical author, but he was much more sensitive to social abuse than William Makepeace Thackeray, and responded readily to the concerns of the Condition of England Question.

The Condition of England

One example of Dickens's ideal world and two of his darker visions in Phiz's illustrations, which Dickens closely supervised: (a) *Christmas Eve at Mr. Wardle's.* Two scenes in debtor's prison: (b) *Mr. Pickwick sits for his Portrait.* (c) *The Warden's Room.* [Click on these images for larger pictures.]

In *The Pickwick Papers* (1837) Dickens created a utopian and nostalgic vision of pre-Victorian and pre-industrial England prior to a rapid industrialisation and urbanisation. Although the novel was designed to be comic, it is not free of Dickens's characteristic social commentary, which would become more pronounced in his later novels. The descriptions of Eatanswill (Chapter 13) and the grim Fleet prison (Chapter 41) anticipate some of Dickens's preoccupations with the Condition of England, which are revealed in his subsequent novels dealing with the darker and more disgusting side of Victorian times. ***The following passage from The Pickwick Papers anticipates Dickens's lifelong concern with the effects of industrialisation on English society.***

It was quite dark when Mr. Pickwick roused himself sufficiently to look out of the window. The straggling cottages by the roadside, the dingy hue of every object visible, the murky atmosphere, the paths of cinders and brick-dust, the deep-red glow of furnace fires in the distance, the volumes of dense smoke issuing heavily forth from high toppling chimneys, blackening and obscuring everything around; the glare of distant lights, the ponderous wagons which toiled along the road, laden with clashing rods of iron, or piled with heavy goods all betokened their rapid approach to the great working town of Birmingham.

As they rattled through the narrow thoroughfares leading to the heart of the turmoil, the sights and sounds of earnest occupation struck more forcibly on the senses. The streets were thronged with working people. The hum of labour resounded from every house; lights gleamed from the long casement windows in the attic storeys, and the whirl of wheels and noise of machinery shook the trembling walls. The fires whose lurid, sullen light had been visible for miles, blazed fiercely up, in the great works and factories of the town. The din of hammers, the rushing of steam, and the heavy clanking of engines was the harsh music which arose from every quarter. [632-33]

Dickens's later novels contain some of his most trenchant pieces of social commentary. Beginning with his second novel, *Oliver Twist*, through *Nicholas Nickleby*, *A Christmas Carol*, *The Chimes*, *Dombey* and *Son*, *Bleak House*, *Hard Times*, and ending with *Little Dorrit*, Dickens totally rejected the claims of classical economics and showed his moral concern for the social well being of the nation. His early novels expose isolated abuses and shortcomings of individual people, whereas his later novels contain a bitter diagnosis of the Condition of England.

Oliver Twist (1837-39), which represents a radical change in Dickens's themes, is his first novel to carry a social commentary similar to that contained in the subsequent Condition-of-England novels. According to Louis Cazamian, "the success of *Twist* confirmed Dickens' determination to write on social topics, and the inception of Chartism. It means, the burning social issue of the day was the problem of the working class " (164). Dickens explores many social themes in *Oliver Twist*, but there are predominant. The abuses of the new Poor Law system, the evils of the criminal world in London and the victimization of children. The critique of the Poor Law of 1834 and the administration of the workhouse is presented in the opening chapters of *Oliver Twist*. Dickens gives the most uncompromising critique of the Victorian workhouse, which was run according to a regime of prolonged hunger, physical punishment, humiliation and hypocrisy.

Dickens succeeded in making Victorian public opinion more aware of the conditions of the poor. He depicted persuasively the disorder, squalor, blight, decay, and the human misery of a modern industrial city. Although the initial condition of England discourse changes into a sentimental moral fable on the subsequent pages, *Oliver Twist* is an important manifestation of Victorian social conscience. The motif of child abuse in the context the Victorian education system is continued in *Nicholas Nickleby* (1838-9). The novel contains a serious social commentary on the conditions of schools where unwanted children were maltreated and starved.

Pale and haggard faces, lank and bony figures, children with the countenances of old men, deformities with irons upon their limbs, boys of stunted growth, and others whose long meager legs would hardly bear their stooping bodies, all crowded on the view together; there were the bleared eye, the hare-lip, the crooked foot, and every ugliness or distortion that told of unnatural aversion conceived by parents for their offspring, or of young lives which, from the earliest dawn of infancy, had been one horrible endurance of cruelty and neglect. There were little faces which should have been handsome, darkened with the scowl of sullen, dogged suffering; there was childhood with the light of its eye quenched, its beauty gone, and its helplessness alone remaining; there were vicious faced boys, brooding, with leaden eyes, like malefactors in a jail; and there were young creatures on whom the sins of their frail parents had descended, weeping even for the mercenary nurses they had known, and lonesome even in their loneliness.

The novel directs this ironical attack at Victorian public opinion, which was either unaware treatment of poor children. Dickens was critical about the Victorian education system which is reflected not only in *Nicholas Nickleby*, *Hard Times* and *Our Mutual Friend*, but also in his journalism and public speeches. As a boy he was shocked to read reports about the cheap boarding schools in the North. In *Nicholas Nickleby* Dickens describes abusive practices in Yorkshire boarding schools. However, Dickens does not only criticize the malicious education system, but he is primarily concerned with the fates of these unfortunate children who are representatives of the most vulnerable portion of the society.

Although Dickens's early works implied faith in the new commercial middle class as opposed to the old aristocracy, the writer saw the discrepancy between the ideas and practice of this new class and the principles of morality and ethic. As a social commentator, Dickens saw the need for the reform of English society; he urged that the wealthy and privileged exhibit a greater humanitarianism towards the poor and the vulnerable.

During the 1850s Dickens's interests shifted gradually from the examination of individual social ills to the examination of the state of society, particularly its laws, education, industrial relations, the terrible conditions of the poor. Increasingly, apart from fictional plots, his novels contained a considerable amount of social commentary similar to Henry Mayhew's nonfictional narratives about the London poor.

Two of Phiz's illustrations for *Bleak House*. (a) Extreme poverty: *The Visit to the Brickmaker's*. (b) Treatment of poor children: *Mr. Chadband 'Improving' a Tough Subject*. [Click on these images for larger pictures.]

Although *Bleak House* (1852-53) is often called England's first authentic contribution to modern detective fiction, it also sharply indicts the inequities in Victorian society. Dickens's finest novel, although not his most popular, it exposes the abuses of the court of Chancery and administrative incompetence. For Dickens, the Court of Chancery became synonymous with the faulty law system, expensive court fees, bureaucratic practices, technicality, delay and inconclusiveness of judgments. Apart from the critique of the Chancery courts, Dickens also criticizes slum housing, overcrowded urban graveyards, neglect of contagious diseases, electoral corruption, preachers; class divisions, and neglect of the educational needs of the poor. The book opens with the famous description of London in fog.

Fog up the river, where it flows among green aims and meadows; fog down the river, where it rolls defiled among the tiers of shipping, and the waterside pollutions of a great (and dirty) city.Fog on the Essex marshes, fog on the Kentish heights. Fog creeping into the cabooses of collier-brigs; fog lying out on the yards, and hovering in the rigging of great ships; fog drooping on the gunwales of barges and small boats. Fog in the eyes and throats of ancient Greenwich pensioners, wheezing by the firesides of their wards; fog in the stem and bowl of the afternoon pipe of the wrathful skipper, down in his close cabin; fog cruelly pinching the toes and fingers of his shivering little prentice boy on deck. Chance people on the bridges peeping over the parapets into a nether sky of fog, with fog all round them, as if they were up in a balloon, and hanging in the misty clouds.

This fog is also very symbolic. It stands for institutional oppression which penetrates into every segment of Victorian society. Dickens sees London as a place of human misery, and the world he perceives is governed by greed and money. *Bleak House* also carries a warning against the excesses of the Laisez-Faire economy. The descriptions of streets, buildings and people are realistic and reflect the living conditions of England in the mid-19th century. The colours in the novel are predominantly grey and black, and the fog becomes one of the central symbols of the novel.

Bleak House provides not only a satirical look at the legal system in England, which often destroys the lives of innocent people, but also offers a vast panorama of Victorian England, which includes the foggy streets of London, filthy slums, the maze of the Inns of Court and also the peaceful countryside, with characters ranging from murderous villains, a "fallen woman" (Lady Deadlock) to virtuous girls and members of landed aristocracy, all of whom are affected by the flaws of the torturous Victorian judiciary system. The atmosphere, places and events are described with great authenticity. In this view *Bleak House* is one of the most important novels about the condition of Victorian society. As Terry Eagleton has noted, "Dickens sees his society as rotting, unraveling, so freighted with meaningless matter that it is sinking back gradually into some primeval slime ".

Bleak House does not merely refer to Mr. Jarndyce's house but also to the Condition of England, which is represented as a "gloomy edifice" and whose judicial system must be reformed if England wants to continue as a modern nation. Dickens describes emphatically urban poverty by the example of the slum street, where poor Jo lives, in a manner similar to the Sanitary Reports. The moral corruption of Chancery is juxtaposed with the physical decay of the slums:

Jo lives in a ruinous place known to the like of him by the name of Tom-all-Alone's. It is a black, dilapidated street, avoided by all decent people, where the crazy houses were seized upon, when their decay was far advanced, by some bold vagrants who after establishing their own possession took to letting them out in lodgings. Now, these tumbling tenements contain, by night, a swarm of misery. As on the ruined human wretch vermin parasites appear, so these ruined shelters have bred a crowd of foul existence that crawls in and out of gaps in walls and boards; and coils itself to sleep, in maggot numbers, where the rain drips in; and comes and goes, fetching and carrying fever and sowing more evil in its every footprint than Lord Coodle, and Sir Thomas Doodle, and the Duke of Foodle, and all the fine gentlemen in office, down to Zoodle, shall set right in five hundred years – though born expressly to do it. Twice lately there has been a crash and a cloud of dust, like the springing of a mine, in Tom-all-Alone's; and each time a house has fallen. These accidents have made a paragraph in the newspapers and have filled a bed or two in the nearest hospital. The gaps remain, and there are not unpopular lodgings among the rubbish. As several more houses are nearly ready to go, the next crash in Tom- all-Alone's may be expected to be a good one. [Ch. 16, 182-183]

Dickens's description of Tom-All-Alone's, a rookery in St Giles, east of Charing Cross Road, can be read both as historical evidence and a powerful literary symbol of the Condition of England, where uncontrolled industrialisation contributed, in Dickens's opinion, to misery, decay and disease. Likewise, Chancery stands as a bitter metaphor of moral corruption which pervades the upper classes. The social consequences of industrialisation and urbanisation are perhaps most persuasively depicted in Hard Times (1854), which Dickens wrote at the prompting of urgent external circumstances. Hard Times is more than any other of his Condition of England novels influenced by Carlyle's social criticism. It deals with a number of social issues: industrial relations, education for the poor, class division and the right of common people to amusement. It also draws on contemporary concern with reforming divorce laws. Cazamian sees Dickens in *Hard Times* as an "intermediary link between the social thought of Carlyle and Ruskin." (173) Raymond Williams described *Hard Times* as "a thorough-going and creative examination of the dominant philosophy of industrialism-of the hardness that Mrs Gaskell saw as little more than a misunderstanding, which might be patiently broken down" (93). Similarly, in his study, "The Rhetoric of Hard Times", David Lodge wrote:

On every page *Hard Times* manifests its identity as a polemical work, a critique of mid-Victorian industrial society dominated by materialism, acquisitiveness, and ruthlessly competitive capitalist economics. To Dickens, at the time of writing *Hard Times*, these things were represented most articulately, persuasively, (and therefore dangerously) by the Utilitarians. [86]

Dickens, like Thomas Carlyle and many other contemporary intellectuals, criticised Utilitarianism, although they confused utilitarian ethics with laissez-faire industrial capitalism, which, like Utilitarianism, was based on the self-interest principle.

In *Hard Times* Dickens created a Condition-of-England novel, which directly engaged with contemporary and social issues. The volume edition of the novel bore the subtitle: "For these Times", which referred to Carlyle's essay of 1829 "Signs of the Times". As Michael Goldberg has pointed out, "Carlyle remained a hero to Dickens throughout his life..." (2), and his critique of Utilitarianism bears a strong affinity with Carlyle's. Carlyle exposed the dangers of a mechanistic and inhuman system which deprived people of such human qualities as emotion, affection and imagination. Dickens echoes many of Carlyle's arguments against the power of social machinery and materialist consciousness. However, contrary to Carlyle, Dickens shows that the positive aspects of human nature are not easily destroyed. Fancy, imagination, compassion and hope do not disappear completely. They are preserved in such characters as Sissy, Rachael and Sleary. Even Mr. Gradgrind revealed eventually some traces of humanness. Ultimately, Dickens did not take up Carlyle's favourite theme of the aristocratic hero as the saviour of a disintegrating society.

Coketown, the city of Fact, foreshadows the emergence of a monstrous mass urban society based on rationalism, anonymity, Dehumanisation. The dominant feature of the town is its inherent ugliness. Its inhabitants lack individuality and are the product of an inhuman, materialistic society.

It was a town of red brick, or of brick that would have been red if the smoke and ashes had allowed it; but as matters stood it was a town of unnatural red and black like the painted face of a savage. It was a town of machinery and tall chimneys, out of which interminable serpents of smoke trailed themselves for ever and ever, and never got uncoiled. It had a black canal in it, and a river that ran purple with ill-smelling dye, and vast piles of building full of windows where there was a rattling and a trembling all day long, and where the piston of the steam engine worked monotonously up and down like the head of an elephant a state of melancholy madness. It contained several large streets all very like one another, and many small streets still more like one another, inhabited by people equally like one another, who all went in and out at the same hours, with the same sound upon the same pavements, to do the same work, and to whom every day was the same as yesterday and to-morrow, and every year the counterpart of the last and the next. [Ch. V,28]

In *Hard* Times human relationships are contaminated by economics. The principles of the 'dismal science' led to the formation of a selfish and atomistic society. *The social commentary of Hard Times is quite clear. Dickens is concerned with the conditions of the urban labourers and the excesses of laissez-faire capitalism. He exposes the exploitation of the working class by unfeeling industrialists and the damaging consequences of propagating factual knowledge (statistics) at the expense of feeling and imagination.* However, Dickens is critical about Utilitarianism, he cannot find a better way of safeguarding social justice than through ethical means."In place of Utilitarianism, Dickens can offer only good-heartedness, individual charity, and Sleary's horse-riding; like other writers on the Condition of England Question, he was better equipped to examine the symptoms of the disease than to suggest a possible cure" (Wheeler, 81).

Hard Times proves that fancy is essential for human happiness, and in this aspect it is one of the best morally uplifting novels. *Dickens avoided propagating employer paternalism in the manner of Disraeli, Charlotte Brontë and Gaskell, and strongly opposed commoditization of labour in Victorian England.* As John R. Harrison has pointed out:

The target of Dickens's criticism, however, was not Bentham's Utilitarianism, nor Malthusian theories of population, nor Smith's free-market economics, but the crude utilitarianism derived from such ideas by Benthamite Philosophical Radicals, which tended to dominate social, political, and economic thinking and policy at the time the novel was written. The Gradgrind/Bounderby philosophy is that the Coketown " Hands" are commodities, " something" to be worked so much and paid so much, to be "infallibly settled" by "laws of supply and demand," something that increased in number by a certain "rate of percentage" with accompanying percentages of crime and pauperism.

Hard Times was in fact an attack on the Manchester School of economics, which supported *laissez*-faire and promoted a distorted view of Bentham's ethics. The novel has been criticised for not offering specific remedies for the Condition-of-England problems it addresses. It is debatable whether solutions to social problems are to be sought in fiction, but nevertheless, Dickens's novel anticipated the future debates concerning anti-pollution legislation, intelligent town-planning, health and safety measures in factories and a humane education system.

Observation

Dickens as a social commentator exerted a profound influence on later novelists committed to social analysis. Some of his concerns with the Condition-of-England Question were further dealt with in the novels of Charles Kingsley, George Eliot, George Gissing, George Orwell, and recently in the postmodern novels of Martin Amis and Zadie Smith.

Dickens and Society

Throughout his career, Dickens protested the abuse of children and the corruption of individual feelings. His portrayal of the destructiveness of society's institutions and values becomes more insistent and savage in his later novels. In his early, hopeful novels, the problems of his protagonists, who are often orphaned or abandoned as children, are solved by the benevolence of good men. Dickens lost faith in the ability of individuals to remedy the unjust treatment of individuals. He perceived that injustice, indifference, and cruelty were pervasive and incorporated into society's institutions.

Because of, Dickens's moral outrage and his attacks on society's institutions and values, later critics, who were often Marxists, hailed him variously subversive, rebellious, and even revolutionary. They did not necessarily claim that Dickens was aware of the subversion or revolutionary thrust of his novels. George Bernard Shaw compared Marx and Dickens. Thus, "The difference between Marx and dickens was that Marx knew he was a revolutionist whilst Dickens had not the faintest suspicion of that part of his calling." There was good reason for contrasting the two men; Marx fled to London in 1849, died there in 1883, and was also a writer. Thus, the two men were observing the same society and class structure; both were subject to similar social conditions and pressures. Furthermore, *Barnaby Rudge* and *A Tale of*

Two Cities both are set in revolutionary times, identify some of the abuses that sparked the outbreaks, and describe the violent, chaotic behavior of the mobs.

George Orwell, in 1946, viewed Dickens's "rebelliousness" from a different perspective:

In *Oliver Twist, Hard Times, Bleak House, Little Dorrit,* Dickens attacked English institutions with a ferocity that has never since been approached. Yet he managed to do it without making him hated, and, more than this, the very people he attacked have welcomed him. Hence, he completely has become a national institution himself.

We cannot express our conviction that it is to the fact that he represents a class that he owes his speedy elevation to the top of the wave of popular favor. He is a man of very liberal sentiments and assailer of constituted wrongs and authority's one of the advocates in the plea of Poor versus Rich, to the progress of which he has lent no small aid in his day. But, he perhaps more distinctly than any other author of his time, a class writer, the historian and representative of one circles in the many ranks in our social scale. Despite, their descents into the lowest class, and their occasional flights into the less familiar ground of fashion, it is the air and breath of middle-class respectability which fills the books of Mr. Dickens.

Unlike Thackeray, Dickens was not seen as quite or fully a gentleman. Thackeray's province was, as W.C. Roscoe described it, "the debatable land between the aristocracy and the middle classes". Dickens showed the efforts of the lower strata of the middle class to rise from being tradesmen and upper servants into the respectable middle classes. Thackeray wrote that "an English gentleman knows as much about the people of Lapland or California as he does of the aborigines of the Seven Dials or the natives of Whapping." Dickens knew, and wrote with sympathy and understanding, about the classes who lived in such neighborhoods as Seven Dials and Whapping. Furthermore, Dickens was accused of being unable to describe a gentleman. G. K. Chesterton explained that this accusation really meant that Dickens could not describe a gentleman as gentlemen feel a gentleman. He described them from the outside, as he described any other oddity or special trade.

Bleak House based on Some Critical Approaches in Analysis based on Marxism Criticism

Bleak House is a novel written by Charles Dickens. Charles Dickens was born on February 7, 1812, in Hampshire, England, and spent the first ten years of his life in Kent. When Dickens was ten, the family moved to London. His father, a naval pay clerk was a spend thrift and eventually lost all the family's money, sending him, his wife, and their eight children to debtors' prison. When Dickens was twelve, his mother forced him to live apart from the family by himself for three months, at which time he worked at a blacking factory (blacking is a kind of soot used to create black pigment for such products as matches and boots) to help support the family. Along with the other children at the factory, Dickens pasted labels on bottles, an experience he hated and one that affected him deeply throughout his life. His experiences at the factory, as well as his family's experiences with poverty and debt, spurred a passionate interest in social issues and reform. When his father was released from prison, Dickens returned to school. He eventually became a law clerk but abandoned law to become a journalist. This proved to be the start of a lifetime of writing he published his first story in 1833 and his first novel, The Pickwick Papers, in 1836, when he was just twenty-five years old. The novel was very highly regarded and launched Dickens's celebrity as a writer.

Dickens was a prolific writer and published novels roughly every two years. After The Pickwick Papers, he published Oliver Twist (1837) and Nicholas Nickel by (1838). Dickens usually published his novels in serial form in magazines, several chapters at a time, and the serialized pieces were then published together as a novel. Bleak House, Dickens's ninth novel, was published in twenty installments between March 1852 and September 1853. In 1850, Dickens founded the journal Household Words and became its editor, intent on using the journal to promote social reform. Along with political articles, he published fiction to give the journal wider appeal, including his own novel Hard Times (1854). In 1859, he quit Household Words and began editing All the Year Round. Like Household Words, All the Year Round addressed social issues and featured both fiction and nonfiction. Dickens serialized several of his novels in All the Year Round, including A Tale of Two Cities (1859) and Great Expectations (1860-1861)

Marxist and Dickens: Great Expectations from Money and Class Mobility

In *The Communist Manifesto*, "Bourgeois and Proletarians" is subtitled by Friedrich Engels and Karl Marx as such: "The history of all society till now is the history of class struggles". The division between what Engels and Marx define as the proletariat and bourgeois classes of society begins after the end of feudalism with the birth of private ownership. One particular, interesting aspect of which is social mobility. After private ownership, as long as a person had money they were capable of elevating themselves to another class. The character Pip in *Great Expectations* by Charles Dickens is a classic example of a man whose social status transformed solely due to money, which contributed to the alienation of his being, as well as eventually leading him to a realization of class consciousness. Pip, the blacksmith's apprentice, goes from a lower class boy in the countryside to a gentleman in London high society. Although, Pip did not achieve any class mobility through his own labour, but rather through the capital of an anonymous benefactor. Finally, Pip later comes to learn his benefactor is a former criminal named Magwitch whom he encountered years ago as a boy. In Marxist terms, the money changed Pip's social identity and at the same time alienated him from his own being. He did nothing to actually earn the money. Therefore the alienation Pip experience is more severe. However, in the end Pip does realize his own self-deceit. Pip is "at last compelled to confront soberly (his) situation in life, (his) relations to others" (*The Communist Manifesto* 65). Only through his move between classes and back again is Pip capable of awakening to the reality of life class is merely a divisive social construct.

Class mobility was made more possible after the death of feudalism by the emergence of private ownership. However, as Marx states in *The Communist Manifesto*, "the modern bourgeois society that has sprouted from the ruins of feudal society has not done away with class antagonism. But he has established new classes, new conditions of oppression, new forms of struggle in place of the old ones" . Therefore, an individual can move between classes, but at a price; both a monetary one, as well as one of a social nature. This is evident in the entirety of *Great Expectations*, as we read along while Pip goes from proletariat to a hobnobbing with the upper crust of London society in university studies and smoking rooms. Through the journey of Pip, we see how these new divisions in class are no less oppressive than those during the previous period of feudalism. The first time Pip truly realizes the difference between classes is after his first encounters with Miss Havisham and Estella at Satis House.

As part of the bourgeois class who inherited land and wealth from her father, Miss Havisham begins to negatively shape Pip's conception of his own social status as a "common labouring-boy" (Dickens 60). She literally embodies the bourgeoisie in Marxist terms by staying in her old wedding dress for years and letting the house around her deteriorate, as "in bourgeois society… the past dominates the present" (*The Communist Manifesto* 76). After he initially visits Satis House, his want to become a 'gentleman' grows. In the presence of Miss Havisham, Pip sees the life of leisure. For instance, unlike at the marsh with Joe in the forge, Miss Havisham does nothing except 'play', as she calls it (Dickens 58). First, he laments the job working with Joe as a blacksmith, proclaiming it dirty and harsh work after experiencing the leisurely days at Satis House. At the same time, Pip does not turn his back on Joe yet and still admires him for being a hard working man. However, once the young protege of Miss Havisham, Estella, starts asserting an influence on Pip he worries. The thought of Estella seeing him do the work of the proletariat is upsetting. Pip believes if she were to ever witness this she would never talk to or want to see him again. He sees himself not as "distinguished and happy" like he once thought working for Joe would make him feel, and instead feels "dusty with the dust of small-coal with a weight upon (him) daily remembrance to which the anvil was a feather" (Dickens 107). Therefore, the influence of both Miss Havisham and Estella grow on Pip, their bourgeoisie lives seducing him, and his former proletariat mind is then warped. From this point on, Pip becomes obsessed with class mobility and seeks to push his way upward into the bourgeoisie.

The snobbish Mr. Jaggers arrives soon after Pip starts spending time at Satis House to announce a wealthy benefactor wishing to fund his move between classes. Funnily enough, the boy assumes it is Miss Havisham, which makes him feel important and thrusts him into a transition. In his new upper class life Pip finds himself far removed from work. Marx believed labour was a good thing only as long as "the relation of the worker to the product of labour" (*Economic and Philosophic Manuscripts of 1844* 74) remains free of alienation. In the newly industrialized world of the late 18th century and into the middle of the 19th century, many people were alienated from the fruits of their labour. Briefly say, the labourers in factories and cotton mills using machinery were producing "wonderful things" for the bourgeois, those who own the means of production; for the workers, this only meant "privation" as they became more like machines themselves (*Economic and Philosophic Manuscripts of 1844* 73). Given a sum of money with which to transform himself into a gentleman, Pip is completely alienated from the activity of labour. Pip makes his way using money he did not earn. There is no personal meaning to his capital, he is alienated even from the money through which he enters into a higher class. "In bourgeois society capital is independent and has individuality, while the living person is dependent and has no individuality" (*The Communist Manifesto* 76). Therefore, it is the money which basically moves independently between classes while Pip is dependent on it for everything, robbing him of personhood. Later in the novel, Pip begins to lament the fact he had not "risen to manhood content to be partners with Joe in the *honest* old forge". With Joe, making a living was honest, and the money he earned would have given him more personal pride, more a sense of himself and his identity. Whereas the money Magwitch provides him only serves to alienate him from the class in which he was born, his true needs, the people around him and, effectively, the common man, or the proletariat. In addition, Pip finds a totally new world opened up to him due to money. Pip imagines that his anxieties may be assuaged by means of capital: "If I could have kept (Joe) away by paying money, I certainly would have paid money" (Dickens 218). The social relationships between Pip and others are alienated, just as Pip finds himself alienated from his own being. Subsequently, Pip's alienation is reversed through seeing Joe once again and discovering Magwitch as his anonymous benefactor. (Dickens 272)

Engels and Marx view written history as the history of class struggle. In similar fashion, as does Pip's former mentor Joe Bargery believe the world works in such terms: "Life is made of ever so many partings welded together. Divisions among such must come, and must be met as they come" (Dickens 224). Perhaps the most visible instance of a recognition of class divisions comes when Pip is visited by Joe at his new place in London. Even before when Pip went back to visit at his old home in the marsh, Dickens did not impart such an intense recognition by any of the characters. However, once Joe and his perceived common identity come to London it is as if Pip is confronted with his old life in such a blatant juxtaposition. Joe himself recognizes this well enough, as he tells Pip: "I'm wrong in these clothes. I'm wrong out of the forge, the kitchen, or off th'meshes. You won't find half so much fault in me if you think of me in my forge dress" (Dickens 224). Joe has essentially succumbed to the expectations of society and plays the part of the class to which he supposedly belongs. His identity is completely bound up in his work, his designation as proletariat. Without the proper clothes of his trade, he does not even feel normal or right, but rather he is uncomfortable and perceives himself as a out of place. In opposition, Pip does recognize he is from a lower class, though, he aims to act and appear as part of the bourgeoisie. One of the only ways Pip will relate back to the world of the blacksmith he experienced is through a classical piece by Handel: the Harmonious Blacksmith (Dickens 179). Otherwise, Pip is reluctant to even acknowledge his previous social life at the marsh with Joe. In fact, he and Joe have an unpleasant meeting later when the latter goes to London and meets with Pip. The newly bourgeoisie Pip is ashamed of his former life as a blacksmith's apprentice. Having Joe in his presence only exacerbates these feelings of shame and pushes Pip further into the mindset of the bourgeoisie. The great expectations of Dickens' title come to bear on Pip who confronts what is expected of him, as a member of the upper class. Because of this he begins to reject Joe and his old status of blacksmith apprentice. On the contrary, once Pip discovers the identity of his mysterious benefactor this prompts him to face his own newly formed prejudice as an upper class gentleman.

Magwitch, formerly a member of the lumpenproletariat, somehow tears himself from those moorings and gains capital, which Marx defines as "accumulated labour"(*Economic and Philosophic Manuscripts of 1844* 98). Marx saw the lumpenproletariat as a group which will never attain class consciousness and are technically unuseful to any kind of social production. Less amicably, Marx saw them as the "passive putrifying of the lowest layers of old society" (*The Communist Manifesto* 72). However, Magwitch defies this definition due to his unusual class consciousness. In fact, it is his desire to strike back at the ruling class which drives him to work, in order to pay for Pip's education as a gentleman. On one hand, Magwitch helped Pip. On the other hand, Marx might disagree. It is through the mysterious donation of Magwitch that Pip becomes alienated from his being. Nevertheless, if the former criminal had not helped Pip move from proletariat to bourgeoisie, the latter may never have reached a point of respective class consciousness. Pip's journey towards becoming a 'gentleman' has taken him full circle and brought him back to the lower class.

Even the title of Charles Dickens' *Great Expectations* demands a particular interpretation. Social class comes along with certain expectations forced upon individuals: how to appear and how to present oneself based on financial status. In his own life Dickens dealt with the disparity between the rich and the poor, or in Marxist terms, the gap between the proletariat and bourgeoisie. The industrial revolution and the emergence of capitalism brought about class mobility, which was not at all common during the days of feudalism. Through the character of Pip, and to a lesser extent the criminal Magwitch, Dickens explored how a member of the Marxian proletariat was able to make his way into the bourgeoisie. However, Pip experiences the inner struggle of rejecting his given social status and those in his former social sphere. By the end of the novel Pip's experience as a member of the bourgeoisie ultimately helped him towards a realization of class consciousness. It took Pip leaving the marshes and entering into city society for him to realize, as Marx writes in the *Grundrisse der Kritik der Politischen Ökonomie*: "The human being is in the most literal sense a political animal, not merely a gregarious animal, but an animal which can individuate itself only in the midst of society" (223). Essentially, this transition from proletariat to bourgeoisie was necessary in order for Pip to wake from a sleep of ignorance and helps him finally comprehend the idea of class as a socially constructed system of division between individuals. (C.H. Newell)

Russian Literature

The unusual shape of Russian literary history has been the source of numerous controversies. Three major and sudden breaks divide it into four periods-pre-Petrine (or Old Russian), Imperial, post-Revolutionary, and post-Soviet. The reforms of Peter I (the Great; reigned 1682–1725), who rapidly Westernized the country, created so sharp a divide with the past that it was common in the 19th century to maintain that Russian literature had begun only a century before. The 19th century's most influential critic, Vissarion Belinsky, even proposed the exact year (1739) in which Russian literature began, thus denying the status of literature to all pre-Petrine works. The Russian Revolution of 1917 and the Bolshevik coup later in the same year created another major divide, eventually turning "official" Russian literature into political propaganda for the communist state. Finally, Mikhail Gorbachev's ascent to power in 1985 and the collapse of the U.S.S.R. in 1991 marked another dramatic break. What is important in this pattern is that the breaks were sudden rather than gradual and that they were the product of political forces external to literary history itself.

From the 14th to the 17th Century

Moscow's Ascendancy

Beginning in the 1230s, the Tatars conquered most of the Russian lands, thus destroying the hegemony of Kiev and initiating a period in which political and cultural power was dispersed among numerous principalities. Eventually the grand princes of Moscow succeeded in defeating the Tatars (1480) and subduing the principalities. (The exception was the lands under the rule of the Lithuanian-Polish kingdom, and this division initiated the development of separate Ukrainian and Belarusian cultural traditions.) Once the Russian lands were united, Tsar Ivan IV (Ivan the Terrible; reigned 1533–84) undertook a campaign against the remaining power of the old aristocracy (boyars). Reflecting these political facts, chronicles and saints' lives served the interests of particular local powers. A series of works in various genres, known as the Kulikovo cycle, celebrated the first (but by no means definitive) Russian victory over the Tatars in 1380 under the leadership of Grand Prince Dmitry Ivanovich ("Donskoy"). A rather weak imitation of the Igor Tale, the *Zadonshchina* (attributed to Sofony of Ryazan and composed no later than 1393) glorifies Dmitry Donskoy.

The Second South Slavic Influence

The Ottoman occupation of the Balkans at the end of the 14th century, and later the conquest of Constantinople in 1453, drove a number of prelates to Russia, thus initiating the "Second South Slavic Influence." Schooled in an Eastern Christian theological movement, Hesychasm, these men brought with them a style of writing closely linked to their theological doctrines. Known as "word weaving," this ornamental style played with phonic and semantic correspondences. It appears in the most notable hagiography of the period, *Zhitiye svyatogo Sergiya Radonezhskogo* ("Life of Saint Sergius of Radonezh") by Epifany Premudry (Epiphanius the Wise; d. between 1418 and 1422).

Possessors and Non Possessors

A theological and political controversy of great significance took place between St. Joseph of Volokolamsk (1439–1515) and his followers, known as the "Possessors," or "Josephites," and

Nil Sorsky (1433–1508) and his followers, known as the "Nonpossessors." Joseph justified the killing of heretics and the church's possession of lands (thus the name "Possessors"). These positions were disputed by Nil and his followers, especially Vassian Patrikeyev (d. before 1545) and Maximus the Greek (*c.* 1475–1556). The Nonpossessors called for greater tolerance and an inner, more spiritual religion, a view that left its mark on a tradition eventually embodied in Dostoyevsky's ideal monk, Father Zosima, in his novel *The Brothers Karamazov*. With the Josephites' triumph, the division between church and state dissolved; apostasy and treason became inseparably linked.

Works Reflecting Muscovite Power

Accompanying Moscow's rise were a series of writings on the theme of *translatio imperii* ("translation of empire"), which constructed genealogies and described the transmission of imperial and ecclesiastical regalia to Russia. Particularly important is the monk Philotheus' (Filofei's) epistle to Vasily III (written between 1514 and 1521), which proclaimed that, with the fall of Constantinople (the second Rome), Moscow became the third (and last) Rome. Along with the title tsar (caesar) and the claim that Orthodox Russia was the only remaining true Christian state, the doctrine of the Third Rome came to justify Russian imperial ambitions and to legitimize the idea that it was Russia's destiny to save and rule the world.

Reflecting the consolidation of Muscovite power were a series of encyclopaedic works, including the enormous *Velikiye Minei-Cheti* ("Great Martyrologue") of 1552, the *Ulozheniye* ("Code of Laws"), and other collections or codifications. Encyclopaedic writing also includes the famous *Domostroy*, or rules for household management, which later became a byword for oppressive narrow-mindedness. The 16th century also saw the first examples of polemical writing by laymen. Ivan Peresvetov (rather superfluously) urged Ivan the Terrible to inspire fear. From a literary point of view, the most remarkable work of this period is the correspondence between Andrey Mikhaylovich, Prince Kurbsky (1528–83) and Ivan the Terrible. In a series of letters Kurbsky, who escaped from Russia and entered the service of the Polish king, denounced Ivan's tyrannical rule and developed a theory justifying rebellion against unjust power. In a simple but polemically powerful style, which included citations from Cicero, he also denounced Russian cultural backwardness, thus earning a reputation as Russia's first "Westernizer" (as well as first "dissident" and first "émigré" writer). In his vituperative replies, Ivan exhibits the psychology of a victim (self-pitying in accounts of his childhood) turned victimizer. Among the other noteworthy works of this period are some tales of entertainment, including *Povest o Petre i Fevroni* (mid-16th century; "Tale of Peter and

Fevroniya"). In his *Khozhdeniye za tri morya* ("Journey Beyond Three Seas") a merchant, Afanasy Nikitin, describes his travels to India and Persia during 1466–72. However, what is most striking about this period is what did not take place: Russia experienced no Renaissance and became quite isolated from the West. With nothing resembling Western secular literature, philosophy, or science, it remained a land remarkable for its lacks.

The 17th Century

The 17th century began with a period of political chaos. The ruling Muscovite dynasty came to an end in 1598. Before Michael Romanov was at last proclaimed tsar in 1613, Russia was convulsed by struggles for power, peasant rebellions, and foreign invasions. This Time of Troubles became the topic of a number of historical or memoiristic works, including Avraamy Palitsyn's *Istoriya v pamyat sushchim predydushchim godom* (completed in 1620; "History to Be Remembered by Future Generations").

Western cultural influences gradually penetrated Russia in the 17th century. They entered the country through a number of channels, including the "German [foreign] quarter" in Moscow and through Ukraine, which was united with Russia in 1654. Ukrainian and Belarusian clerics, who had received a Polish-style education at the Kiev Academy, brought Western and Latin culture with them to Moscow. By the end of the 17th century, Russian literature had changed in important ways. A key figure in producing these changes was Simeon Polotsky (1629–80), a monk educated at the Kiev Academy. He played the leading role in introducing syllabic poetry (verse that is measured by the number of syllables in each line), based on Polish models, into Russia. Old Russian literature had been dominated entirely by prose, and so Polotsky's verse marked a decisive break. So did the introduction of drama into Russia with Polotsky's school dramas (modeled on Jesuit Counter-Reformation plays having biblical or religious themes), the establishment of a court theatre by Tsar Alexis, and the production of *Artakserksevo deystvo* (1672; "Action of Artaxerxes"), the first court play (in prose), by Johann Gottfried Gregory. The change in literary culture is also evident in the beginnings of prose fiction. Translations of foreign adventure romances appeared, along with Russian stories, parodies, and satires, including the picaresque (and erotic) *Povest o Frole Skobeyeve* ("Tale of Frol Skobeyev") and *Kalyazinskaya chelobitnaya* ("The Kalyazin Petition"). *Povest o Gore-Zlochastii* ("Tale of Woe-Misfortune"), written in folk-epic verse, combines motifs of temptation, adventure, and salvation.

In the mid-17th century liturgical reforms undertaken by Patriarch Nikon split the Russian church. The dissenters (or Old Believers) produced some remarkable work, including the masterpiece of 17th-century Russian writing *Zhitiye protopopa Avvakuma* (1672–73; *The Life of the Archpriest Avvakum*). Avvakum, who eventually was burned at the stake, narrates his life in a powerful vernacular alternating with Church Slavonicisms. Written in prison, his narrative conveys a feel for his fanatic, earthy personality in a paradoxical form that is both autobiography and autohagiography.

The "Ukrainian hegemony" over Russian letters continued during the reign of Peter I the Great. St. Dmitry (Tuptalo) of Rostov, Stefan Yavorsky, and Feofan Prokopovich, the three most important writers of the period, were all educated at the Kiev Academy.

Imperial Literature

The Westernization of Russia

Peter the Great's radical and rapid Westernization of Russia altered the daily life of the upper classes and all high culture. The nobility was made to conform to Western models in its dress, customs, social life, education, and state service; women came out of seclusion; a European calendar was introduced; Russians were sent abroad to study; foreign languages were learned. Western culture was absorbed so rapidly in the course of the 18th century that by the 19th century the first language of the upper nobility was not Russian but French. As a result, a large cultural gap opened between the nobility and the peasantry, whose distance from each other became an important theme of Russian literature. In the context of world history, Russia may be seen as the first of many countries to undergo rapid modernization and Westernization while wrestling with a question capable of different answers: in adopting Western technology and science, is it also necessary to adopt Western culture and forms of living? Under Peter's autocratic will, Russia was forced into an uncompromisingly affirmative answer to this question, which has concerned Russian writers up to the present moment.

In 1703 Peter founded a new capital, St. Petersburg. It was built in Western architectural style and populated by his command on an inhospitable swamp. The city-Peter's "window to the West"-became a key theme of literary works, including Aleksandr Pushkin's poem *The Bronze Horseman*, Dostoyevsky's novel *Crime and Punishment*, and Andrey Bely's novel *St. Petersburg*. In contrast to Moscow, St. Petersburg came not only to symbolize the power of the state over the individual but also to stand for reason and planning divorced from tradition, individual human needs, and the nonrational elements of human nature. The hero of Dostoyevsky's *Notes from the Underground* calls the capital the world's "most artificial city," associating it with utopian contempt for tradition and experience. Like Peter's reforms generally, the city evoked the idea of historical change by sudden leaps rather than by a gradual, organic process.

The Response of Writers and Critics

By the 19th century it became commonplace to regard Russia as a young country that had entered history only with the Petrine reforms. The very genres in which 19th-century literature was written had essentially no counterpart in medieval Russia, deriving instead from European literary history. Thus, in tracing their literary past, Russians often felt the necessity of "crossing borders." To be sure, it became common for Russian writers to appropriate old Russian themes, characters, and events, as is the case in Pushkin's *Boris Godunov*, Mikhail Lermontov's *Pesnya pro kuptsa Kalashnikova*, and Tolstoy's *Father Sergius*. But these works are recognizably conscious of overcoming a break. Some scholars have insisted that the idea of a radical break in Russian literary history is mistaken, but there is no doubt that the perception of discontinuity is a key fact of Russian literary history.

An aura of foreignness adhered to high culture, which is one reason why a tradition arose in which the sign of Russianness was the defiance of European generic norms. Justifying the self-consciously odd form of *War and Peace*, Tolstoy observed that departure from European form is necessary for a Russian writer: "There is not a single work of Russian artistic prose, at all rising above mediocrity, that quite fits the form of a novel, a poem, or a story." This (admittedly exaggerated) view, which became a cliché, helps explain the enormous popularity in Russia of those Western writers who parodied literary conventions, such as the 18th-century British novelist Laurence Sterne, as well as the development of Russia's most influential school of literary criticism, Formalism, which viewed formal self-consciousness as the defining quality of "literariness." The sense that culture, literature, and the forms of "civilized" life were a foreign product imported by the upper classes is also reflected in a tendency of Russian thinkers to regard all art as morally unjustifiable and in a pattern of Russian writers renouncing their own works. While English and French critics were arguing about the merits of different literary schools, Russian critics also debated whether literature itself had a right to exist-a question that reveals the peculiar ethos of Russian literary culture.

The 18th Century

The 18th century was a period of codification, imitation, and absorption of foreign models. The century's major contribution was the development of a literary language. Under the pressure of new subject matter and the influx of foreign expressions, Church Slavonic proved inadequate, and the resulting linguistic chaos required the standardization of literary Russian.

In 1758 Mikhail Lomonosov published "Predisloviye o polze knig tserkovnykh v rossiyskom yazyke" ("Preface on the Use of Church Books in the Russian Language") in which he classified Russian and Church Slavonic words, assigning their use to three styles, and correlated these styles with appropriate themes, genres, and tones. Thus the Russian literary language was to be established by a combination of Russian and Church Slavonic.

Verse also changed decisively. The old syllabic verse, based on qualities of the Polish language, gave way to syllabotonic verse (*i.e.*, verse in which the number of stressed syllables in each line becomes the dominant prosodic element), more suitable to Russian. Theories of versification were advanced by Vasily Trediakovsky in 1735 and 1752 and, especially, by Lomonosov in 1739 (the date Belinsky chose as the beginning of Russian literature). It is also noteworthy that the Petrine assault on the church decisively ended the role of the clergy in Russian literature.

Throughout the 18th century Russian writers imitated, adapted, and experimented with a wide variety of European genres, thus grafting them onto the Russian tradition and making them available for later, more original, use. Much classical and western European literature was translated, read, and assimilated, thus producing a kind of telescopic effect, as works and movements that were centuries apart were absorbed at the same time. Four writers dominate the period from the death of Peter to the ascension of Catherine II the Great in 1762. Antiokh Kantemir is best known for his verse satires. In addition to his treatises and poems in various genres, Trediakovsky produced a poetic psalter. Lomonosov, who was also a scientist and played a key role in founding Moscow State University (1755), achieved his greatest poetic success in panegyric and spiritual odes, especially "Oda na vzyatiye Khotina" (1739; "Ode on the Seizure of Khotin"), "Vecherneye razmyshleniye o Bozhiyem velichestve" (1743; "Evening Meditation on the Majesty of God"), and "Utrenneye razmyshleniye o Bozhiyem velichestve" (1743; "Morning Meditation on the Majesty of God"). Whereas Baroque poetics strongly influenced Trediakovsky and Lomonosov, the younger Aleksandr Sumarokov, a poet and dramatist, stood for a rigorous and lucid classicism.

Catherine II the Great

Catherine began her reign as an enlightened despot. She corresponded with Voltaire and Denis Diderot and sponsored the arts. Although her native language was German, she has to her credit a number of plays in Russian as well as a statement of legal principles, *Nakaz* (*Instruction*). In 1769 she established a satiric journal, *Vsyakaya vsyachina* ("All Sorts and Sundries"), which was soon followed by others, including the *Truten* ("Drone"), founded by

Nikolay Novikov. In a curious exchange between journals, Novikov and Catherine disagreed with each other about the nature of satire-like the Kurbsky-Ivan correspondence in the 16th century, it was a case of a sovereign deigning to argue with a subject. Shocked by an uprising of Cossacks and peasants (1773–75), known from the name of its leader as the Pugachov Rebellion, and later by the French Revolution, Catherine turned increasingly conservative. Generally speaking, these events marked a turning point as the Russian autocracy switched from being a modernizing to a restraining force. When Aleksandr Radishchev published *Puteshestviye iz Peterburga v Moskvu* (1790; *A Journey from St. Petersburg to Moscow*), a work that was sharply critical of Russian society and serfdom, Catherine had him condemned to death, a sentence she commuted to Siberian exile. Offended by a posthumously published play by Yakov Knyazhnin (1742–91), *Vadim Novgorodsky* ("Vadim of Novgorod"), she had copies of the manuscript burned and the published text torn from the offending volume.

Poetry

Catherine's reign saw real accomplishment in Russian poetry. Excellent verse was produced, and the canon as it is known today began to take shape. It is worth stressing the important role of tradition and the canon in Russian poetry. To a much greater extent than in many other traditions, including the English and American, Russian poetry typically relies on the reader's detailed knowledge of earlier poems. The poems of the past constitute a sort of literary bible, a common culture known in detail by the literate public. Poets count on their readers being sufficiently familiar with the tradition to detect even faint allusions to earlier poems. Moreover, Russian poets also rely on readers to appreciate the semantic associations that specific verse forms have acquired, which is perhaps one reason why free (unrhymed and unmetered) verse has played a relatively small role in Russian poetry.

Three poets-Ivan Khemnitser, Ivan Dmitriyev, and Ivan Krylov-are known for their fables. Krylov's fables rapidly became classics and some of his lines proverbial. *Rossiyada* (written 1771–79; "The Rossiad"), an epic by Mikhail Kheraskov, is a rather stilted effort that proved a literary dead end. It was the ode, rather than the epic, that was the successful high poetic genre of the age. But Vasily Maykov and Ippolit Bogdanovich wrote amusing mock epics. Maykov's *Elisey; ili, razdrazhenny Vakkh* (1769; "Elisei; or, Bacchus Enraged") cleverly parodies a Russian translation of the *Aeneid* with a narrative in which the Greek pantheon directs whores, drunks, and other low-lifes. In *Dushenka: drevnyaya povest v volnykh stikhakh* (1783; "Dushenka: An Ancient Tale in Free Verse"), Bogdanovich produced a light and witty updating of the Greek myth of Cupid and Psyche.

Gavrila Derzhavin is generally considered to be Russia's greatest 18th-century poet. He is best known for his odes, including his chatty panegyric "Oda k Felitse" (1782; "Ode to Felitsa"), in which praise for the prosaic virtues of Empress Catherine alternates with depictions of the low amusements of courtiers. His poems "Bog" (1784; "God") and "Vodopad" (1791–94; "The Waterfall") daringly make the metaphysical concrete and the specific poetic. Derzhavin, who also served as a governor and as Catherine's personal secretary, exemplifies the tendency of 18th-century writers to pursue government careers, a practice that was almost unthinkable a century later.

Drama and Prose Fiction

Although the theatrical repertoire in the late 18th and early 19th centuries continued to be dominated by translations and adaptations, numerous, if not very distinguished, tragedies were written by Sumarokov, Kheraskov, Vladislav Ozerov, and others. Of greater merit were two comedies by Denis Fonvizin, *Brigadir* (1769; *The Brigadier*), a satire on Gallomania, and *Nedorosl* (1783; "The Minor"). Prose fiction began to appear in print only in the mid-18th century. Mikhail Chulkov's picaresque *Prigozhaya povarikha* (1770; "The Comely Cook") is addressed to a popular audience. At the end of the 18th century, the dominant figure of Russian sentimentalism was Nikolay Karamzin, author of *Pisma russkogo puteshestvennika* (1792; *Letters of a Russian Traveler, 1789–1790*), describing a journey to western Europe in 1789–90, and of the very popular story "Bednaya Liza" (1792; "Poor Liza"), a tale of lovers separated because they belong to different social classes, which seems cloying to the modern reader. Appointed imperial historiographer, Karamzin later wrote the 12-volume *Istoriya gosudarstva rossiyskogo* (1818–26; "History of the Russian State"), which is a landmark of Russian literature. Karamzin's importance also lies in his contribution to the Russian literary language. His writing reflected the language of high society, using a Gallicized vocabulary and syntax at the expense of Church Slavonic.

The 19th Century

The Russian 19th century is one of the most fruitful periods in world literature. Several features, in addition to those mentioned above, distinguish the literary culture of these years: (1) Literature enjoyed greater prestige in Russia than in the West, and its achievements were sometimes thought (as Dostoyevsky once declared) to be the justification for the Russian people's very existence. Literary critics were typically the leaders of Russian intellectual life and political thought. (2) Literature and criticism were expected to fulfill functions, such as philosophical, moral, and religious analysis, that in Europe were typically assigned to distinct disciplines. Thus Dostoyevsky's works are central to the histories of all these areas of Russian thought. One can see why the highest achievement of Russian literature was probably the philosophical novel. (3) In the 19th (still more, the 20th) century, politics and literature were intimately connected, and a writer or critic was often called upon to be a political prophet.

The "Golden Age" of Poetry

Readers relying on translations usually think of Russian literature almost exclusively in terms of prose, but for Russians their tradition is also, and perhaps equally, one of poetry. The 19th century began with the "Golden Age" of Russian poetry. An aristocratic sensibility, the culture of salons, an aura of friendly intimacy, and genres suitable to this ethos marked the poetry of this period. The romantic poet Vasily Zhukovsky is celebrated for several translations or adaptations that are major poems in their own right, including versions of the English poet Thomas Gray's "An Elegy Written in a Country Church Yard" (1802 and 1839), Homer's *Odyssey* (completed 1847), and Lord Byron's "The Prisoner of Chillon" (1822). His "Svetlana" (1813) reworks the German poet Gottfried August Bürger's "Lenore." Konstantin Batyushkov was noted for playful and erotic as well as melancholy verse and for the elegy *Umerayushchy Tass* (1817; "The Dying Tasso"). The "Pushkin Pleiad," consisting of poets of Pushkin's generation and closely associated with him, included Anton Delvig, Prince Pyotr Vyazemsky, and, most important, Yevgeny Baratynsky, who was a superb philosophical "poet of thought."

Aleksandr Pushkin

Pushkin occupies a unique place in Russian literature. It is not just that Russians view him as their greatest poet; he is also virtually the symbol of Russian culture. His life, as well as his work, has acquired mythic status. To criticize Pushkin, or even one of his characters-as, for example, Tatyana, the heroine of his novel *Yevgeny Onegin* (written 1823–31; *Eugene Onegin*)-has been taken as something akin to blasphemy. Pushkin's quasi-sacred status has itself been parodied by Russian authors, including the satirist Mikhail Zoshchenko, the absurdist Daniil Kharms, and, most recently, Andrey Sinyavsky in his *Progulki s Pushkinym* (1972; *Strolls with Pushkin*).

Even if, one sets this mythic image aside, Pushkin is truly one of the world's most accomplished poets; his verse, however, which relies on the author's perfect control of form, tone, and language, does not read well in translation. Deeply playful and experimental, Pushkin adopted a vast array of conflicting masks and personae. He wrote now seriously with irony, and now with irony at his own irony, on moral and philosophical themes. He is ultimately a philosophical fox, appreciating the limitations, as well as the virtues, of any set of ideas. A master parodist, Pushkin wrote a number of erotic and at times sacrilegious mock-epics, such as "Gavriiliada" (1821)

Lermontov and Griboyedov

Next to Pushkin, Mikhail Lermontov, who personifies Romanticism, is probably Russia's most frequently anthologized poet. His celebrated lyrics often recycle lines from his own and others' poems. "Smert poeta" (1837; "Death of a Poet"), which first earned him fame, deals with Pushkin's death shortly after a fatal duel in 1837. Among his narrative poems, *Demon* (1841; *The Demon*) describes the love of a Byronic demon for a mortal woman; *Pesnya pro tsarya Ivana Vasilyevicha, molodogo oprichnika i udalogo kuptsa Kalashnikova* (1837; *A Song About Tsar Ivan Vasilyevich, His Young Bodyguard, and the Valiant Merchant Kalashnikov*) is a stylized folk epic. Also an accomplished prose stylist, Lermontov wrote *Geroy nashego vremeni* (1840; *A Hero of Our Time*), which in form is something between a novel and a complexly framed cycle of stories about a single hero, a Byronic superfluous man. This work ranges from sketches of philosophical brilliance ("The Fatalist") to episodes of near puerility ("Princess Mary"). The theme of the superfluous man finds another important rendition in Aleksandr Griboyedov's classic work, *Gore ot uma* (completed 1824; *Woe from Wit*).

Nikolay Gogol

One of the finest comic authors of world literature, and perhaps its most accomplished nonsense writer, Gogol is best known for his short stories, for his play *Revizor* (1836; *The Inspector General*, or *The Government Inspector*), and for *Myortvye dushi* (1842; *Dead Souls*), a prose narrative that is nevertheless subtitled a "poem." "Nos" (1836; "The Nose"), a parable on the failure of all explanatory systems, relates an utterly inexplicable incident and the attempts to come to terms with it. Both "Shinel" (1842; "The Overcoat"), which is probably the most influential Russian short story, and "Zapiski sumasshedshego" (1835; "The Diary of a Madman") mix pathos and mockery in an amazing display. As in "Nevsky prospekt" (1835; "Nevsky Avenue") and "Povest o tom, kak possorilsya Ivan Ivanovich s Ivanom Nikiforovichem" (1835; "The Tale of How Ivan Ivanovich Quarrelled with Ivan Nikiforovich"), language itself seems to generate its own absurd content while the universe turns out to be a counterfeit of which there is no original. Characteristic of Gogol is a sense of boundless superfluity that is soon revealed as utter emptiness and a rich comedy that suddenly turns into metaphysical horror. *The Inspector General* develops a sequence of (witting and unwitting) confidence games within confidence games in a corrupt world of endless self-deception. The mock-epic, even mock-satiric, *Dead Souls* simultaneously allegorizes the timeless bureaucratic tendency to make official documentation more genuine than actual existence, the emptiness of the human soul, and the mind's absurd ways of grasping meaning or value. It is one of the most striking (and most Gogolian) ironies of Russian literary history that radical critics celebrated Gogol as a realist.

Other Poets and Dramatists

From the death of Lermontov until the end of the 19th century, Russian literature was dominated by prose, but some poets of lasting interest appeared. Fyodor Tyutchev, a member of Pushkin's generation, wrote nature, love, and political poetry but is probably best appreciated for his philosophical "poetry of thought," including "Silentium!" (1830). Afanasy Fet wrote delicate love lyrics remarkable for their absence of verbs. Violently attacked by radical critics as symbolizing pure art, he came to be appreciated by the Symbolist poets to follow. Nikolay Nekrasov, who was also a major figure in Russian journalism, wrote social satires, tendentious "civic" verse, and compassionate accounts of peasant life, including *Komu na Rusi zhit khorosho?* (1879; *Who Can Be Happy and Free in Russia?*), which he began writing in 1863 and left unfinished at the time of his death.

Among the dramatists of this period, Aleksandr Ostrovsky, who has proved much more popular in Russia than abroad, wrote many slice-of-life plays about the Russian merchantry. His plays *Svoi lyudi-sochtyomsya!* (1850; "It's a Family Affair-We'll Settle It Among Ourselves"; Eng. trans. *A Family Affair*) and *Groza* (1859; *The Thunderstorm*) were the subject of reviews by Nikolay Dobrolyubov (1836–61), one of Russia's most influential radical critics. Aleksandr Sukhovo-Kobylin wrote a macabre trilogy, whose third play, *Smert Tarelkina* (1869; *The Death of Tarelkin*), is a brilliant piece of grotesque humour about a man who fakes his own death. The theme of the faked suicide, a motif of Russian drama, later appeared in Leo Tolstoy's *Zhivoy trup* (written 1900; *The Living Corpse*) and Nikolay Erdman's *Samoubiytsa* (1928; *The Suicide*).

Leo Tolstoy

Probably even more than Dostoyevsky, Tolstoy has been praised as being the greatest novelist in world literature. The 19th-century English critic and poet Matthew Arnold famously expressed the commonest view in saying that a work by Tolstoy is not a piece of art but a piece of life: his novels read as if life were writing directly, without mediation. Tolstoy's techniques reflect his belief that no theory is adequate to explain the world's complexity, which unfolds by "tiny, tiny alterations" fitting no pattern. He denied the existence of historical laws and insisted that ethics is a matter not of rules but of supreme sensitivity to the particular. "True life," he contended, is lived not at moments of grand crisis but at countless ordinary and prosaic moments, which human beings usually do not notice. All these ideas are illustrated and explicitly expressed in *Voyna i mir* (1865–69; *War and Peace*), set in the time of the Napoleonic wars, and in *Anna Karenina* (1875–77), which applies this prosaic view of life to marriage, the family, and work. *Anna Karenina* also contrasts romantic love, which is based on intense moments of passion and leads to adultery, with the prosaic love of the family, which is based above all on intimacy.

After completing *Anna Karenina,* Tolstoy underwent a religious crisis, which eventually led him to reject his two great novels, formulate a new religion that he thought of as true Christianity, and cultivate a different type of art. To outline his views, he wrote a number of tracts, including *Tsarstvo bozhiye vnutri vas* (1893; *The Kingdom of God Is Within You*) and *Chto takoye iskusstvo?* (1898; *What Is Art?*). His only long novel of this period, *Voskreseniye* (1899; *Resurrection*), is a tendentious failure. But he produced brilliant novellas, many of which were published posthumously, including *Otets Sergy* (written 1898; *Father Sergius*), in which he seems to reflect on his own quest for sainthood, and *Khadzhi-Murat* (written 1904; *Hadji-Murad*).

Ivan Turgenev

The first Russian writer to be widely celebrated in the West, Turgenev managed to be hated by the radicals as well as by Tolstoy and Dostoyevsky for his dedicated Westernism, bland liberalism, aesthetic elegance, and tendency to nostalgia and self-pity. He first gained fame with his subtle descriptions of peasant life in *Zapiski okhotnika* (1852; *A Sportsman's Sketches*), which contributed to the climate leading to the abolition of serfdom. He is celebrated for his novels about *intelligent*s and ideology: *Rudin* (1856), *Nakanune* (1860; *On the Eve*), and *Dym* (1867; *Smoke*). His most distinguished work, *Ottsy i deti* (1862; *Fathers and Sons*), offers both an evenhanded portrait of the radical nihilists and an allegorical meditation on the conflict of generations.

Anton Chekhov

When Tolstoy abandoned the prosaic ethos, Chekhov, one of the greatest short story writers in world literature, remained loyal to it. Indeed, he reinterpreted it within his essentially bourgeois values, stressing the moral necessity of ordinary virtues such as daily kindness, cleanliness, politeness, work, sobriety, paying one's debts, and avoiding self-pity. Replying to the intelligentsia's demand for political tendentiousness, which he equated with a stifling intellectual conformity, he maintained that his only "tendency" was a protest against lying in all its forms. In his hundreds of stories and novellas, which he wrote while practicing medicine, Chekhov adopts something of a clinical approach to ordinary life. Meticulous observation and broad sympathy for diverse points of view shape his fiction. In his stories, an overt plot subtly hints at other hidden stories, and so the experience of rereading his fiction often differs substantially from that produced by a first reading. Especially noteworthy are "Skuchnaya istoriya" (written 1889; "A Dreary Story"), "Duel" (written 1891; "The Duel"), "Palata No. 6" (written 1892; "Ward Number Six"), "Kryzhovnik" (written 1898; "Gooseberries"), "Dushechka" (written 1899; "The Darling"), "Dama s sobachkoy" (written 1899; "The Lady with the Lap Dog"), "Arkhiyerey" (written 1902; "The Bishop"), and "Nevesta" (written 1903; "The Betrothed").

The Silver Age

The period from the 1890s to 1917 was one of intellectual ferment, in which mysticism, aestheticism, Neo-Kantianism, eroticism, Marxism, apocalypticism, Nietzscheanism, and other movements combined with each other in improbable ways. Primarily an age of poetry, it also produced significant prose and drama. Russian Symbolism, which was influenced by French Symbolist poetry and the philosophy of Vladimir Solovyov (1853–1900), is usually said to have begun with an essay by Dmitry Merezhkovsky, "O prichinakh upadka i o novykh techeniyakh sovremennoy russkoy literatury" (1893; "On the Reasons for the Decline and on the New Trends in Contemporary Russian Literature"). A poet and propagator of religious ideas, Merezhkovsky wrote a trilogy of novels, *Khristos i Antikhrist* (1896–1905; *Christ and Antichrist*), consisting of *Yulian otstupnik* (1896; *Julian the Apostate*), *Leonardo da Vinchi* (1901; *Leonardo da Vinci*), and *Pyotr i Aleksey* (1905; *Peter and Alexis*), which explores the relation of pagan and Christian views of the world.

Symbolists

The Symbolists saw art as a way to approach a higher reality. The first wave of Symbolists included Konstantin Balmont (1867–1942), who translated a number of English poets and wrote verse that he left unrevised on principle (he believed in first inspiration); Valery Bryusov (1873–1924), a poet and translator of French Symbolist verse and of Virgil's *Aeneid*, who for years was the leader of the movement; Zinaida Gippius (1869–1945), who wrote decadent, erotic, and religious poetry; and Fyodor Sologub, author of melancholic verse and of a novel, *Melky bes* (1907; *The Petty Demon*), about a sadistic, homicidal, paranoid school teacher.

Three writers dominate the second wave of Symbolism. Eschatology and anthroposophy shaped the poetry and prose of Andrey Bely, whose novel *Peterburg* (1913–22; *St. Petersburg*) is regarded as the masterpiece of Symbolist fiction. Aleksandr Blok, who wrote the lyric drama *Balaganchik* (1906; "The Showbooth"), is best known for his poem *Dvenadtsat* (1918; *The Twelve*), which describes 12 brutal Red Guards who turn out to be unwittingly led by Jesus Christ. The principal theoretician of the Symbolist movement, Vyacheslav Ivanov (1866–1949), wrote mythic poetry conveying a Neoplatonist philosophy.

Acmeists and Futurists

In the second decade of the 20th century, Symbolism was challenged by two other schools, the Acmeists, who favoured clarity over metaphysical vagueness, and the brash Futurists, who wanted to throw all earlier and most contemporary poetry "from the steamship of modernity." Among the Acmeists, Nikolay Gumilyov (1886–1921), who stressed poetic craftsmanship over the occult, was executed by the Bolsheviks. Already an accomplished creator of superb love lyrics in these years, Anna Akhmatova produced densely and brilliantly structured poems in the Soviet period, including *Poema bez geroya* (written 1940–62; *A Poem Without a Hero*) and *Rekviyem* (written 1935–40; *Requiem*), which was inspired by Soviet purges and was therefore unpublishable in Russia. From 1923 to 1940 she was forced into silence, and in 1946 Akhmatova and Zoshchenko became the target of official abuse by the Communist Party cultural spokesman Andrey Zhdanov (1896–1948). Some consider Osip Mandelshtam (1891–1938), who died in a Soviet prison camp, to be the greatest Russian poet of the 20th century. Many of his difficult, allusive poems were preserved by his wife, Nadezhda Mandelshtam (1899–1980), whose memoirs are themselves a classic.

The two most important Futurist poets were Velimir Khlebnikov and Vladimir Mayakovsky. Khlebnikov hoped to find the laws of history through numerology and developed amazingly implausible theories about language and its origins. His verse, which is characterized by neologisms and "trans-sense" language, includes "Zaklyatiye smekhom" (1910; "Incantation by Laughter") and *Zangezi* (1922). Mayakovsky epitomized the spirit of romantic bohemian radicalism. Humour, bravado, and self-pity characterize his inventive long poems, including *Oblako v shtanakh* (1915; *A Cloud in Trousers*). After the Russian Revolution in 1917, which he ardently supported initially, Mayakovsky "stepped on the throat" of his song to produce propaganda poems. But he also satirized Soviet bureaucracy in the witty "Razgovor s fininspektorom o poezii" (1926; "Conversation with a Tax Collector about Poetry"). As a dramatist, he is best known for *Vladimir Mayakovsky* (1913), in which he played the lead role, and *Klop* (1929; *The Bedbug*), in which a philistine, along with a bedbug, is resurrected into the banal communist future of 1979. Having written a poem about the suicide of the peasant poet Sergey Yesenin (1895–1925), Mayakovsky later shot himself, leaving a brilliantly ironic suicide note with a poem explaining that "love's boat has smashed against daily life."

CHAPTER - V

LABOUR TRANSITION AND GLOBAL ISSUES

The Spontaneity of the Masses and the Consciousness of the Social-Democrats

Our movement, much more extensive and deep than the movement of the seventies, must be inspired with the same devoted determination and energy that inspired the movement at that time. Indeed, we think that no one has until now doubted that the strength of the present-day movement lies in the awakening of the masses (principally, the industrial proletariat) and that its weakness lies in the lack of consciousness and initiative among the revolutionary leaders. However, of late a staggering discovery has been made, which threatens to disestablish all prevailing views on this question. This discovery was made by *Rabocheye Dyelo*, which in its polemic with *Iskra* and *Zarya* did not confine itself to making objections on separate points, but tried to ascribe "general disagreements" to a more profound cause to the "different appraisals of the *relative* importance of the spontaneous and consciously 'methodical' element". *Rabocheye Dyelo* formulated its indictment as a *"belittling of the significance of the objective or the spontaneous element of development"*.

The Beginning of the Spontaneous Upsurge

Theories of Marxism in the middle of the nineties have made strikes that followed the famous St. Petersburg industrial war of 1896 assumed a similar general character. Their spread over the whole of Russia clearly showed the depth of the newly awakening popular movement, and if we are to speak of the "spontaneous element" then, it is this strike movement which, first and foremost, must be regarded as spontaneous. But there is spontaneity and spontaneity. Strikes occurred in Russia in the seventies and sixties (and even in the first half of the nineteenth century), and they were accompanied by the "spontaneous" destruction of machinery, etc. Compared with these "revolts", the strikes of the nineties might even be described as "conscious", to such an extent do they mark the progress which the working-class movement made in that period. This shows that the "spontaneous element", in essence, represents nothing more nor less than consciousness in an *embryonic form*. Even the primitive revolts expressed the awakening of consciousness to a certain extent. The workers were losing their age-long faith in the permanence of the system which oppressed them and began. The necessity for collective resistance, definitely abandoning their slavish submission to the authorities. But this was more in the nature of outbursts of desperation and vengeance than of *struggle.* The strikes of the nineties revealed far greater flashes of consciousness; definite demands were advanced, the strike was carefully timed, known cases and instances in other places were discussed, etc. The revolts were simply the resistance of the oppressed, whereas the systematic strikes represented the class struggle in embryo, but only in embryo. Taken by themselves, these strikes were simply trade union struggles, not yet Social Democratic struggles. They marked the awakening antagonisms between workers and employers; but the workers were not and could not be conscious of the irreconcilable antagonism of their interests to the whole of the modern political and social system, i.e., there was not yet Social-Democratic consciousness. In this sense, the strikes of the nineties, despite the enormous progress they represented as compared with the "revolts', remained a purely spontaneous movement. There could not have been Social-Democratic consciousness among the workers. It would have to be brought to them from without. The history of all countries shows that the working class, exclusively by its own effort, is able to develop only trade union consciousness, i.e., the conviction that it is necessary to combine in unions, fight the employers, and strive to compel the government to pass necessary labour legislation, etc. The theory of socialism, however, grew out of the philosophic, historical, and economic theories elaborated by educated representatives of the propertied classes, by intellectuals. By their social status the founders of modern scientific socialism, Marx and Engels, themselves belonged to the bourgeois intelligentsia. In the same way, in Russia, the theoretical doctrine of Social-Democracy arose altogether independently of the spontaneous growth of the working-class movement; it arose as a natural and inevitable outcome of the development of thought among the revolutionary socialist intelligence.

In the middle nineties, this doctrine not only represented the completely formulated programme of the **Emancipation of Labour group**, but had already won over to its side the majority of the revolutionary youth in Russia. Hence, we had both the spontaneous awakening of the working masses, their awakening to conscious life and conscious struggle, and a revolutionary youth, armed with Social-Democratic theory and straining towards the workers. In this connection, it is particularly important to state the oft-forgotten (and comparatively little-known) fact that, although the *early* Social-Democrats of that period *zealously carried on economic agitation* (being guided in this activity by the truly useful indications contained in the pamphlet *On Agitation*, then still in manuscript), they did not regard this as their sole task. On the contrary, *from the very beginning* they set for Russian Social-Democracy the most far-reaching historical tasks, in general, and the task of overthrowing the autocracy, in particular fact. Thus, towards the end of 1895, the St. Petersburg group of Social-Democrats, which founded the League of Struggle for the Emancipation of the Working Class, prepared the first issue of a newspaper called *Rabocheye Dyelo*. This issue was ready to go to press when it was seized by the gendarmes, on the night of December 8, 1895, in a raid on the house of one of the members of the group, Anatoly Alexeyevich Vaneyey. The failure of the enterprise merely showed that the Social-Democrats of that period were unable to meet the immediate requirements of the time owing to their lack of revolutionary experience and practical training. This must be said, too, with regard to the *S. Peterburgsky Rabochy Listok* and particularly with regard to Rabochaya Gazeta and the *Manifesto* of the Russian Social-Democratic Labour Party, founded in the spring of 1898. Of course, we would not dream of blaming the Social Democrats of that time for this unpreparedness. But in order to profit from the experience of that movement, and to draw practical lessons from it, we must thoroughly understand the causes and significance of this or that shortcoming. It is therefore highly important to establish the fact that a part (majority) of the Social-Democrats, active in the period of 1895-98, justly considered it possible even then, at the very beginning of the "spontaneous" movement, to come forward with a most extensive programme and a militant tactical line. Lack of training of the majority of the revolutionaries, an entirely natural phenomenon, could not have roused any particular fears. Once the tasks were correctly defined, once the energy existed for repeated attempts to fulfill them, temporary failures represented only part misfortune. Revolutionary experience and organizational skill are things that can be acquired, provided the desire is there to acquire them, provided the shortcomings are recognized, which in revolutionary activity is more than half-way towards their removal. But, what was only part misfortune became full misfortune when this consciousness began to grow dim (it was very much alive among the members of the groups mentioned), when there appeared people–and even Social-Democratic organs–that were prepared to regard shortcomings as virtues, that even tried to invent a *theoretical* basis for their *slavish cringing before spontaneity*. It is time to draw conclusions from this trend, the content of which is incorrectly and too narrowly characterized as Economism.

Bowing to Spontaneity. Rabochaya MYSL

Before dealing with the literary manifestation of this subservience to spontaneity, we should like to note the following characteristic fact (communicated to us from the above-mentioned source), which throws light on the conditions in which the two future conflicting trends in Russian Social-Democracy arose and grew among the comrades working in St. Petersburg. In the beginning of 1897, just prior to their banishment, A.A. Vaneyev and several of his comrades attended a private meeting at which "old" and "young members of the League of' Struggle for the Emancipation of the Working Class gathered. The conversation centered chiefly about the question of organisation, particularly about the "rules for the workers' mutual benefit fund", which, in their final form, were published in *"Listok" Rabotnika,* p. 46. Sharp differences immediately showed themselves between the "old" members ("Decembrists", as the St. Petersburg Social Democrats jestingly called them) and several the "young" members (who subsequently took an active part in the work of *Rabochaya Mysl*), with a heated discussion ensuing. The "young" members defended the main principles of the rules in the form in which they were published. The "old" members contended that the prime necessity was not this, but the consolidation of the League of Struggle into an organisation of revolutionaries to which all the various workers' mutual benefit funds, students' propaganda circles, etc., should be subordinated. It goes without saying that the disputing sides far from realised at the time that these disagreements were the beginning of a cleavage; on the contrary, they regarded them as something isolated and casual. But this fact shows that in Russia, Economist did not arise and spread without a struggle against the "old" Social-Democrats (which the Economists of today are apt to forget). This struggle has not left "documentary" traces behind it, it is *solely* because the membership of the circles then functioning underwent such constant change that no continuity was established and, consequently, differences in point of view were not recorded in any documents. The founding of *Rabochaya Mysl* brought Economism to the light of day, but not at one stroke. We must picture to ourselves concretely the conditions for activity and the short-lived character of the majority of the Russian study circles (a thing that is possible only for those who have themselves experienced it) in order to understand how much there was of the fortuitous in the successes and failures of the new trend in various towns, and the length of time during which neither the advocates nor the opponents of the "new" could make up their minds–and literally had no opportunity of so doing – as to whether this really expressed a distinct trend or merely the lack of training of certain individuals.

After stating that the arm of the "blue-coats" could never halt the progress of the working class movement, the leading article goes on to say: "The virility of the working-class movement is due to the fact that the workers themselves are at last taking their fate into their own hands, and out of the hands of the leaders"; this fundamental thesis is then developed in greater detail. Actually, the leaders (i.e.,. the Social-Democrats, the organisers of the League of Struggle) were, one might say, torn out of the hands of the workers by the police; yet it is made to appear that the workers were fighting against the leaders and liberated themselves from their yoke! Instead of sounding the call to go forward towards the consolidation of the revolutionary organisation and the expansion of political activity, the call was issued for a *retreat* to the purely trade union struggle. It was announced that "the economic basis of the movement is eclipsed by the effort never to forget the political ideal", and that the watchword for the working-class movement was "Struggle for economic conditions" or, better still, "The workers for the workers". It was declared that strike funds "are more valuable to the movement than a hundred other Organisations" (compare this statement made in October 1897, with the polemic between the "Decembrists" and the young members in the beginning of 1897), etc. Catchwords like "We must concentrate, not on the 'cream' of the workers, but on the 'average', mass worker"; "Politics always obediently follows economics", etc., etc., became the fashion, exercising an irresistible influence upon the masses of the youth who were attracted to the movement but who, in the majority of cases, were acquainted only with such fragments of Marxism as were expounded in legally appearing publications.

Political consciousness was completely overwhelmed by spontaneity – the spontaneity of the "Social-Democrats" who repeated Mr. V. V.'s "ideas", the spontaneity of those workers who were carried away by the arguments that a kopek added to a ruble was worth more than any socialism or politics, and that they must "fight, knowing that they are fighting, not for the sake of some future generation, but for themselves and their children" (leader in *Rabochaya Mysl*, No.1). Phrases like these have always been a favourite weapon of the West-European bourgeois, who, in their hatred for socialism, strove (like the German *"Sozial-Politiker"* Hirsch) to transplant English trade-unionism to their native soil and to preach to the workers that by engaging in the purely trade union21 struggle they would be fighting for themselves and for their children, and not for some future generations with some future socialism. And now the "V. V.s of Russian Social-Democracy" have set about repeating these bourgeois phrases. It is important at this point to note three circumstances that will be useful to our further analysis of *contemporary* differences. In the first place, the overwhelming of political consciousness by spontaneity, to which we referred above, also took place *spontaneously*. This may sound like a pun, but, it is the bitter truth. It did not take place as a result of an open struggle between two diametrically opposed points of view, in which one triumphed over the other; it occurred because of the fact that an increasing number of "old" revolutionaries were "torn away" by the gendarmes and increasing numbers of "young" "V.V.s of Russian Social Democracy" appeared on the scene. Everyone, who has, at least breathed the atmosphere of, the *present-day* Russian movement, knows perfectly well that this is precisely the case. And if, nevertheless, we insist strongly that the reader be fully clear on this generally known fact, if we cite, for explicitness, as it were, the facts of the first edition of *Rabocheye Dyelo* and of the polemic between the "old" and the "young" at the beginning of 1897, we do this because the people who vaunt their "democracy" speculate on the ignorance of these facts on the part of the broad public (or of the very young generation).

Secondly, in the very first literary expression of Economism we observe the exceedingly curious phenomenon–highly characteristic for an understanding of all the differences prevailing among presentday Social Democrats–that the adherents of the "labour movement pure and simple", worshippers of the closest "organic" contacts (*Rabocheye Dyelo*'s term) with the proletarian struggle, opponents of any non-worker intelligentsia (even a socialist intelligentsia), are compelled, in order to defend their positions, to resort to the arguments of the *bourgeois* "pure trade-unionists". This shows that from the very outset *Rabochaya Mysl* began – unconsciously – to implement the programme of the *Credo*. This shows (something *Rabocheye Dyelo* cannot grasp) that *all* worship of the spontaneity of the working class movement, all belittling of the role of "the conscious element", of the role of Social-Democracy, *means, quite independently of whether he who belittles that role desires it or not, a strengthening of the influence of bourgeois ideology upon the workers.* All those who talk about "overrating the importance of ideology" about exaggerating the role of the conscious element, etc., imagine that the labour movement pure and simple can elaborate, and will elaborate, an independent ideology for itself, if only the workers "wrest their fate from the hands of the leaders". But this is a profound mistake. To supplement what has been said above, we shall quote the following profoundly true and important words of Karl. Kautsky on the new draft programme of the Austrian Social-Democratic Party. "Many of our revisionist critics believe that Marx asserted that economic development and the class struggle create, not only the conditions for socialist production, but also, and directly, the *consciousness* of its necessity. And these critics assert that England, the country most highly developed capitalistically, is more remote than any other from this consciousness Judging by the draft, one might assume that this allegedly orthodox Marxist view, which is thus refuted, was shared by the committee that drafted the Austrian programme. In the draft programme it is stated: The more capitalist development increases the numbers of the proletariat, the more the proletariat is compelled and becomes fit to fight against capitalism. The proletariat becomes conscious of the possibility and of the necessity for socialism. In this connection socialist consciousness appears to be a necessary and direct result of the proletarian class struggle. But this is absolutely untrue. Of course, socialism, as a doctrine, has its roots in modern economic relationships just as the class struggle of the proletariat has latter, emerges from the struggle against the capitalist-created poverty and misery of the masses. But socialism and the class struggle arise side by side and not one out of the other; each arises under different conditions. Modern socialist consciousness can arise only on the basis of profound scientific knowledge. Indeed, modern economic science is as much a condition for socialist production as, say, modern technology, and the proletariat can create neither the one nor the other, no matter how much it may desire to do so; both arise out of the modern social process. The vehicle of science is not the proletariat, but the *bourgeois intelligentsia* It was in the minds of individual members of this stratum that modern socialism originated, and it was they who communicated it to the more intellectually developed proletarians who, in their turn, introduce it into the proletarian class struggle where conditions allow that to be done. Thus, socialist consciousness is something introduced into the proletarian class struggle from without and not something that arose within it spontaneously. Accordingly, the old Hainfeld programme quite rightly stated that the task of Social-Democracy is to imbue the proletariat (literally: saturate the proletariat) with the *consciousness* of its position and the consciousness of its task. There would be no need for this if consciousness arose of itself from the class struggle. The new draft copied this proposition from the old programme, and attached it to the proposition mentioned above. But this completely broke the. line of thought." Since there can be no talk of an independent ideology formulated by the working masses themselves in the process of their movement, the only choice is – either bourgeois or socialist ideology. There is no middle course (for mankind has not created a "third" ideology, and, moreover, in a society torn by class antagonisms there can never be a non-class or an above-class ideology). Hence, to belittle the socialist ideology *in any way, to turn aside from it in the slightest degree* means to strengthen bourgeois ideology. There is much talk of spontaneity. But the *spontaneous* development of the working-class movement leads to its subordination to bourgeois ideology, *to its development along the lines of the Credo programme;* for the spontaneous working-class movement is trade-unionism, is *Nur-Gewerkschaftlerei,* and trade unionism means the ideological enslavement of the workers by the bourgeoisie. Hence, the task of Social-Democracy, is to combat *spontaneity, to divert* the working-class movement from this spontaneous, trade-unionist striving to come under the wing of the bourgeoisie, and to bring it under the wing of revolutionary Social Democracy.

A fierce struggle against spontaneity was necessary and only after such a struggle, extending over many years were it possible to convert the working population of Berlin from a bulwark of the progressions' party into one of the finest strongholds of Social-Democracy. This struggle is by no means over even today (as might seem to those who learn the history of the German movement from Prokopovich, and its philosophy from Struve). Even now the German working class is to speak, split up among a number of ideologies. A section of the workers is organised in Catholic and monarchist trade unions; another section is organised in the Hirsch-Duricker unions, founded by the bourgeois worshippers of English trade-unionism; the third is organised in Social-Democratic trade unions. The last-named group is immeasurably more numerous than the rest, but the Social-Democratic ideology was able to achieve this superiority, and will be able to maintain it, only in an unswerving struggle against all other ideologies. But why, the reader will ask, does the spontaneous movement, the movement along the line of least resistance, lead to the domination of bourgeois ideology? For the simple reason that bourgeois ideology is far older in origin than socialist ideology, that it is more fully developed, and that it has at its disposal *immeasurably* more means of dissemination. And the younger the socialist movement in any given country, the more vigorously it must struggle against all attempts to entrench non-socialist ideology, and the more resolutely the workers must be warned against the bad counselors who shout against "overrating the conscious element", etc. The authors of the Economist letter, in unison with *Rabocheye Dyelo*, inveigh against the intolerance that is characteristic of the infancy of the movement. It must become imbued with intolerance against those who retard its growth by their subservience to spontaneity. Nothing is so ridiculous and harmful as pretending that we are "old hands" who have long ago experienced all the decisive stages of the struggle. Thirdly, the first issue of Rabochaya Mysl shows that the term "Economism" (which, of course, we do not propose to abandon, since, in one way or another, this designation has already established itself) does not adequately convey the real character of the new trend. *Rabochaya Mysl* does not altogether repudiate the political struggle; the rules for a workers' mutual benefit fund published in its first issue contain a reference to combating the government. *Rabochaya Mysl* believes, however, that "politics always obediently follows economics"(*Rabocheye Dyelo* varies this thesis when it asserts in its programme that "in Russia more than in any other country, the economic struggle is *inseparable* from the political struggle"). *If by politics is meant Social-Democratic politics,* then the theses of Rabochaya and *Rabocheye Dyelo* are utterly incorrect.

The economic struggle of the workers are very often connected (although not inseparably) with bourgeois politics, clerical politics, etc., as we have seen. *Rabocheye Dyelo*'s theses are correct, if by politics is meant trade union politics, viz., the common striving of all workers to secure from the government measures for alleviating the distress to which their condition gives rise, but which do not abolish that condition, i.e., which do not remove the subjection of labour to capital. That striving indeed is common to the English trade-unionists, who are hostile to socialism, to the Catholic workers, to the "Zubatov" workers, etc. There is politics and politics. Thus, *Rabochaya Mysl* does not so much deny the political struggle, as it bows to its *spontaneity*, to its unconsciousness. While fully recognizing the political struggle (better: the political desires and demands of the workers), which arises spontaneously from the working-class movement itself, it absolutely refuses *independently to work out* a specifically *Social-Democratic politics* corresponding to the general tasks of socialism and to Present day conditions in Russia.

The Self-Emancipation Group and Rabocheye Dyelo

"Social-Democracy does not, tie its hands, it does not restrict its activities to someone preconceived plan or method of political struggle; it recognizes all means of struggle as long as they correspond to the forces at-the disposal of the Party," etc. (*Iskra*, No. 1.) and the proposition:"Without a strong organisation skilled in waging political struggle under all circumstances and at all times, there can be no question of that systematic plan of action, illumined by firm principles and steadfastly carried out, which alone is worthy of the name of tactics"(*Iskra*, No. 4)

The confound recognition, *in principle*, of all means of struggle, all plans and methods, provided they are expedient, with the demand *at a given political moment* to be guided by a strictly observed plan is tantamount, if we are to talk of tactics, to confounding the recognition by medical science of various methods of treating diseases with the necessity for adopting a certain definite method of treatment for a given disease. The point is, that *Rabocheye Dyelo*, itself the victim of a disease which we have called bowing to spontaneity, refuses to recognized any "method of treatment" for that disease. Hence, it has made the remarkable discovery that "tactics-as-plan contradicts the fundamental spirit of Marxism" (No. 10, p. 18), that tactics are *"a process of growth of Party tasks, which grow together with the Party"* (p. 11, *Rabocheye Dyelo*'s italics). This remark has every chance of becoming a celebrated maxim, a permanent monument to the *Rabocheye Dyelo* "trend". To the question, whither? the leading organ replies: Movement is a process of changing the distance between the starting-point and subsequent points of the movement. This matchless example of profundity is not merely a curiosity (where it that, it would not be worth dealing with at length), but *the programme of a whole trend*, the very programme which R. M. (in the *"Separate Supplement"* to *Rabochaya*) expressed in the words: That struggle is desirable which is possible, and the struggle which is possible is that which is going on at the given moment. This is precisely the trend of unbounded opportunism, which passively adapts itself to spontaneity. "Tactics-as-plan contradicts the essence of Marxism!" But this is a slander of Marxism; it means turning Marxism into the caricature held up by the Narodniks in their struggle against us. It means belittling the initiative and energy of class-conscious fighters, whereas Marxism, on the contrary gives a gigantic impetus to the initiative and energy of the Social-Democrat, opens up for him the widest perspectives, and (if one may so express it) places at his disposal the mighty force of many millions of workers "spontaneously" rising for the struggle. The entire history of international Social-Democracy teems with plans advanced now by one, now by another political leader, some confirming the far-sightedness and the correct political and organisational views of their authors and others revealing their shortsightedness and their political errors. At the time when Germany was at one of the crucial turning-points in its history. The formation of the Empire, the opening of the Reichstag, and the granting of universal suffrage. Liebknecht had one plan for Social-Democratic politics and work in general, and Schweitzer had another. When the anti-socialist law came down on the heads of the German socialists, Most and Hasselmann had one plan. They began to preach to the Social-Democrats that they themselves had provoked the enactment of the law by being unreasonably bitter and revolutionary, and must now earn forgiveness by their exemplary conduct. There was a third plan, proposed by those who prepared and carried out the publication of an illegal organ. It is easy, with hindsight many years after the struggle over the selection of the path to be followed, and after history has pronounced its verdict as to the expediency of the path selected, to utter profound maxims about the growth of Party tasks, which grow together with the Party. But at a time of confusion, when the Russian "Critics" and Economists are degrading Social-Democracy to the level of trade-unionism, and when the terrorists are strongly advocating the adoption of "tactics-as-plan" that repeats the old mistakes, at such a time, to confine oneself to profundities of this kind, means simply to issue to oneself a "certificate of poverty". At a time when many Russian Social-Democrats suffer from a lack of initiative and energy from an inadequate "scope of political propaganda, agitation, and organisation," from a lack of "plans" for a broader organisation of revolutionary work, at such a time, to declare that "tactics-as-plan" contradicts the essence of Marxism" means not only Marxism in the realm of theory, but *to drag the Party backward* in practice.

Rabocheye Dyelo goes on to sermonise: "The task of the revolutionary Social-Democrat is only to accelerate objective development by his conscious work, not to obviate it or substitute his own subjective plans for this development. *Iskra* knows all this in theory; but the enormous importance which Marxism justly attaches to conscious revolutionary work causes it in practice, owing to its doctrinaire view of tactics, *to belittle the significance of the objective or the spontaneous element of development*" (p. 18). Another example of the extraordinary theoretical confusion worthy of Mr. V. V. and his fraternity. We would ask our philosopher: how many a designer of subjective plans "belittle" objective development? Obviously by losing sight of the fact that this objective development creates or strengthens, destroys or weakens certain classes, strata, or groups, certain nations or groups of nations, etc., and in this way serves to determine a given international political alignment of forces, or the position adopted by revolutionary parties, etc. If the designer of plans did that, his guilt would not be that he belittled the spontaneous element, but, on the contrary, that he belittled the *conscious* element, for he would then show that he lacked the "consciousness" properly to understand objective development. Hence, the very talk of "estimating the *relative* significance" (*Rabocheye Dyelo*'s italics) of spontaneity and consciousness itself reveals a complete lack of "consciousness". If certain "spontaneous elements of development" can be grasped at all by human understanding, then an incorrect estimation of them will be tantamount to "belittling the conscious element". But if they cannot be grasped, then we do not know them, and therefore cannot speak of them. What then is Krichevsky discussing? If he thinks that *Iskra*'s "subjective plans" are erroneous (as he in fact declares them to be), he should have shown what objective facts they ignore, and only then charged *Iskra* with *lacking political consciousness* for ignoring them, with "belittling the conscious element", to use his own words. However, displeased with subjective plans, he can bring forward no argument other than that of "belittling the spontaneous element" he merely shows: that, theoretically, he understands Marxism *a la* Kareyev and Mikhailovsky, who have been sufficiently ridiculed by Beltov; and , practically, he is quite satisfied with the "spontaneous elements of development" that have drawn our legal Marxists towards Bernsteinism and our Social-Democrats towards Economism, and that he is "full of wrath" against those who have determined at all costs *to divert* Russian Social-Democracy from the path of "spontaneous" development. Further, there follow things that are positively droll. "Just as human beings will reproduce in the old-fashioned way despite all the discoveries of natural science, so the birth of a new social order will come about, in the future too, *mainly* as a result of elemental outbursts, despite all the discoveries of social science and the increase in the number of conscious fighters" (p. 19). Just as our grandfathers in their old-fashioned wisdom used to say, Anyone can bring children into the world, so today the "modern socialists "(Nartsis Tuporylov) say in their wisdom, Anyone can participate in the spontaneous birth of a new social order. We too hold that anyone can. All that is required for participation of that kind is *to yield* to Economism.

The greater the spontaneous upsurge of the masses and the more widespread the movement, the more rapid, incomparably so, the demand for greater consciousness in the theoretical, political and organisational work of Social-Democracy. The spontaneous upsurge of the masses in Russia proceeded (and continues) with such rapidity that the young Social Democrats proved unprepared to meet these gigantic tasks. This unpreparedness is our common misfortune, the misfortune of *all* Russian Social-Democrats. The upsurge of the masses proceeded and spread with uninterrupted continuity; it not only continued in the places where it began, but spread to new localities and to new strata of the population (under the influence of the working class movement, there was a renewed ferment among the student youth, among the intellectuals generally, and even among the peasantry). Revolutionaries, however, *lagged behind* this upsurge, both in their "theories" and in their activity; they failed to establish a constant and continuous organisation capable of *leading* the whole movement. We established that *Rabocheye Dyelo* belittled our theoretical tasks and that it "spontaneously" repeated the fashionable catchword "freedom of criticism" those who repeated this catchword lacked the "consciousness" to understand that the positions of the opportunist "Critics" and those of the revolutionaries in Germany and in Russia are diametrically opposed.

How Martynov Rendered Plekhanov More Profound

"What a large number of Social-Democratic Lomonosovs have appeared and" observed a comrade one day, having in mind the astonishing propensity of many who are inclined toward Economism to, arrive, "necessarily, by their own understanding", at great truths (e.g., that the economic struggle stimulates the workers to ponder over their lack of rights) and in doing so to ignore, with the supreme contempt of born geniuses, all that has been produced by the antecedent development of revolutionary thought and of the revolutionary movement. He *arrives at* what was long ago said by Axelrod (of whom our Lomonosov, naturally, says not a word); how, for instance, he is *beginning* to understand that we cannot ignore the opposition of such or such strata of the bourgeoisie (*Rabocheye Dyelo*, No. 9, pp. 61, 62, 71; compare this with Rabocheye Dyelo's Reply to Axelrod, pp. 22, 23-24), etc. and is only "beginning", not more than that, for so little has he understood Axelrod's ideas, that hetalks about "the economic struggle against the employers and the government". For three years (1898-1901) *Rabocheye Dyelo* has tried hard to understand Axelrod, but has so far not understood him! Can one of the reasons be that Social-Democracy, "like mankind", always sets itself only tasks that can be achieved? But the Lomonosovs are distinguished not only by their ignorance of many things (that would be but half misfortune!), but also by their unawareness of their own ignorance. Now this is a real misfortune; and it is this misfortune that prompts them without further ado to attempt to render Plekhanov "more profound". "Much water," Lomonosov-Martynov says, "has flowed under the bridge since Plekhanov wrote his book (*Tasks of the Socialists in the Fight Against the Famine in Russia*). The Social-Democrats who for a decade led the economic struggle of the working class have failed as yet to lay down a broad theoretical basis for Party tactics. This question has now come to a head, and if we should wish to lay down such a theoretical basis, we should certainly have to deepen considerably the principles of tactics developed at one time by Plekhanov. Our present definition of the distinction between propaganda and agitation would have to be different from Plekhanov's (Martynov has just quoted PIekhanov's words: "A propagandist presents many ideas to one or a few persons; an agitator presents only one or a few ideas, but he presents them to a mass of people"). By propaganda we would understand the revolutionary explanation of the present social system, entire or in its partial manifestations, whether that be done in a form intelligible to individuals or to broad masses. By agitation, we would understand the call upon the masses to undertake definite, concrete actions and the promotion of the direct revolutionary intervention of the proletariat in social life."We congratulate Russian-and international-Social-Democracy on having found, thanks to Martynov, a new terminology, more strict and more profound. Hitherto we thought (with Plekhanov, and with all the leaders of the international working class movement) that the propagandist, dealing with, say, the question of unemployment, must explain the capitalistic nature of crises, the cause of their inevitability in modern society, the necessity for the transformation of this society into a socialist society, etc. In a word, he must present "many ideas" indeed, that they will be understood as an integral whole only bya (comparatively) few persons.

The agitator, speaking on the same subject, will take as an illustration a fact that is most glaring and most widely known to his audience say, the death of an unemployed worker's family from starvation and, utilising this fact known to all will direct his efforts to presenting a *single idea* to the "masses", e.g., the senselessness of the contradiction between the increase of wealth and the increase of poverty; he will strive *to rouse* discontent and indignation among the masses against this crying injustice, leaving a more complete explanation of this contradiction to the propagandist. The propagandist requires qualities different from those of the agitator. Kautsky and Lafargue, for example, we term propagandists; Bebel and Guesde we term agitators. To single out a third sphere, or third function, of practical activity, and to include in this function "the call upon the masses to undertake definite concrete actions", is sheer nonsense, because the "call", as a single act, either naturally and inevitably supplements the theoretical treatise, propagandist pamphlet, and agitation speech, or represents a purely executive function. Let us take, for example, the struggle the German Social-Democrats are now waging against the corn duties. The theoreticians write research works on tariff policy, with the "call", say to struggle for commercial treaties and for Free Trade. The propagandist does the same thing in the periodical press and the agitator in public speeches. At the present time the "concrete action" of the masses takes the form of signing petitions to the Reichstag against raising the corn duties. The call for this action comes indirectly from the theoreticians, the propagandists, and the agitators, and, directly, from the workers who take the petition lists to the factories and to private homes for the gathering of signatures. According to the "Martynov terminology", Kautsky and Bebel are both propagandists, while those who solicit the signatures are agitators.

The German example recalled to my mind the German word which literally translated, means "Ballhorning". Johann Ballhorn, a Leipzig publisher of the sixteenth century, published a child's reader in which, as was the custom, he introduced a drawing of a cock, but a cock without spurs and with a couple of eggs lying near it. On the cover he printed the legend, "*Revised* edition by Johann Ballhorn". Ever since then, the Germans describe any "revision" that is really a worsening as "ballhorning". And one cannot help recalling Ballhorn upon seeing how the Martynovs try to render Plekhanov "more profound". Why did our Lomonosov "invent" this confusion? In order to illustrate how *Iskra* "devotes attention only to one side of the case, just as Pleklianov did a decade and a half ago" . "With *Iskra*, propagandist tasks force agitation tasks into the background, at least for the present". If we translate this last proposition from the language of Martynov into ordinary human language (because mankind has not yet managed to learn the newly-invented terminology), we shall get the following: with *Iskra*, the tasks of political propaganda and political agitation force into the background the task of "presenting to the government concrete demands for legislative and administrative measures" that "promise certain palpable results" (or demands for social reforms if we are permitted once again to employ the old terminology of the old mankind not yet grown to Martynov's level).

Political Exposures and "Training in Revolutionary Activity

In advancing against *Iskra* his theory of "raising the activity of the working masses", Martynov actually betrayed an urge *to belittle* that activity, for he declared the very economic struggle before which all economists grovel to be the preferable, particularly important, and "most widely applicable" means of rousing this activity and its broadest field. This error is characteristic, precisely in that it is by no means peculiar to Martynov. In reality, it is possible to "raise the activity of the working masses" *only* when this activity *is not restricted* to "political agitation on an economic basis". A basic condition for the necessary expansion of political agitation is the organisation of *comprehensive* political exposure. *In no way* except by means of such exposures *can* the masses be trained in political consciousness and revolutionary activity.

Hence, activity of this kind is one of the most important functions of international Social-Democracy as a whole, for even political freedom does not in any way eliminate exposures; it merely shifts somewhat their sphere of direction. Thus, the German party is especially strengthening its positions and spreading its influence, thanks particularly to the untiring energy with which it is conducting its campaign of political exposure. Working-class consciousness cannot be genuine political consciousness unless the workers are trained to respond to *all* cases of tyranny, oppression, violence, and abuse, no matter *what class* is affected – unless they are trained to respond from a Social-Democratic point of view and no other. The consciousness of the working masses cannot be genuine class-consciousness, unless the workers learn from concrete, and above all from topical, political facts and events to observe *every* other social class in *all* the manifestations of its intellectual, ethical, and political life; unless they learn to apply in practice the materialist analysis and the materialist estimate of *all* aspects of the life and activity of *all* classes, strata, and groups of the population. Those who concentrate the attention, observation, and consciousness of the working class exclusively, or even mainly, upon itself alone are not Social-Democrats for the self-knowledge of the working class is indissolubly bound up, not solely with a fully clear theoretical understanding–or rather, not so much with the theoretical, as with the practical, understanding of the relationships between *all* the various classes of modern society, acquired through the experience of political life. For this reason the conception of the economic struggle as the most widely applicable means of drawing the masses into the political movement, which our Economists preach, is so extremely harmful and reactionary in its practical significance. In order to become a Social-Democrat, the worker must have a clear picture in his mind of the economic nature and the social and political features of the landlord and the priest, the high state official and the peasant, the student and the vagabond; he must know their strong and weak points; he must grasp the meaning of all the catchwords and sophisms by which each class and each stratum *camouflages* its selfish strivings and its real "inner workings"; he must understand what interests are reflected by certain institutions and certain laws and how they are reflected. But this "clear picture" cannot be obtained from any book. It can be obtained only from living examples and from exposures that follow close upon what is going on about us at a given moment; upon what is being discussed, in whispers perhaps, by each one in his own way; upon what finds expression in such and such events, in such and such statistics, in such and such court sentences, etc., etc. These comprehensive political exposures are an essential and *fundamental* condition for training the masses in revolutionary activity. Why do the Russian workers still manifest little revolutionary activity in response to the brutal treatment of the people by the police, the persecution of religious sects, the flogging of peasants, the outrageous censorship, the torture of soldiers, the persecution of the most innocent cultural undertakings, etc.? Is it because the "economic struggle" does not "stimulate" them to this, because such activity does not "promise palpable results", because it produces little that is "positive"? To adopt such an opinion, we repeat, is merely to direct the charge where it does not belong, to blame the working masses for one's own philistinism (or Bernsteinism). We must blame ourselves, our lagging behind the mass movement, for still being unable to organise sufficiently wide, striking, and rapid exposures of all the shameful outrages. When we do that the most backward worker will understand, *or will feel,* that the students and religious sects, the peasants and the authors are being abused and outraged by those same dark forces that are oppressing and crushing him at every step of his life. Feeling that, he himself will be filled with an irresistible desire to react, and he will know how to hoot the censors one day, on another day to demonstrate outside the house of a governor who has brutally suppressed a peasant uprising, on still another day to teach a lesson to the gendarmes in surplices who are doing the work of the Holy Inquisition, etc. As yet we have done very little, almost nothing, *to bring* before the working masses prompt exposures on all possible issues. Many of us as yet do not recognise this as our *bounden duty* but trail spontaneously in the wake of the "drab everyday struggle", in the narrow confines of factory life. Under such circumstances to say that "*Iskra* displays a tendency to minimise the significance of the forward march of the drab everyday struggle in comparison with the propaganda of brilliant and complete ideas" (Martynov, op. cit., p. 61), means to drag the Party back, to defend and glorify our unpreparedness and backwardness. As for calling the masses to action, that will come of itself as soon as energetic political agitation, live and striking exposures come into play. To catch some criminal red-handed and immediately to brand him publicly in all places is of itself far more effective than any number of "calls"; the effect very often is such as will make it impossible to tell exactly who it was that "called" upon the masses and who suggested this or that plan of demonstration, etc. Calls for action, not in the general, but in the concrete, sense of the term can be made only at the place of action; only those who themselves go into action, and do so immediately, can sound such calls. Our business as Social-Democratic publicists is to deepen, expand, and intensify political exposures and political agitation. A word in passing about "calls to action". The *only newspaper* which *prior* to the spring events *called upon* the workers to intervene actively in a matter that certainly did not *promise* any *palpable results* whatever for the workers, i.e., the drafting of the students into the army, was *Iskra*. Immediately after the publication of the order of January 11, on "drafting the 183 students into the army", *Iskra* published an article on the matter (in its February issue, No. 2), and, *before* any demonstration was begun, forthwith *called upon* "the workers to go to the aid of the students", called upon the "people" openly to take up the government's arrogant challenge.

Our Economists, including *Rabocheye Dyelo*, were successful because they adapted themselves to the backward workers. But the Social-Democratic worker, the revolutionary worker (and the number of such workers is growing) will indignantly reject all this talk about struggle for demands "promising palpable results", etc., because he will understand that this is only a variation of the old song about adding a kopek to the ruble. Such a worker will say to his counsellors from *Rabochaya Mysl* and *Rabocheye Dyelo*: you are busying yourselves in vain, gentlemen, and shirking your proper duties, by meddling with such excessive zeal in a job that we can very well manage ourselves. There is nothing clever in your assertion that the Social-Democrats' task is to lend the economic struggle itself a political character; that is only the beginning, it is not the main task of the Social-Democrats.

The Working Class as Vanguard Fighter for Democracy

We have seen that the conduct of the broadest political agitation and, consequently, of all sided political exposures is an absolutely necessary and a *paramount* task of our activity, if this activity is to be truly Social-Democratic. However, we arrived at this conclusion solely on the grounds of the pressing needs of the working class for political knowledge and political training. But such a presentation of the question is too narrow, for it ignores the general democratic tasks of Social-Democracy, in particular of present-day Russian Social-Democracy. In order to explain the point more concretely we shall approach the subject from an aspect that is "nearest" to the Economist, namely, from the practical aspect. "Everyone agrees" that it is necessary to develop the political consciousness of the working class. The question is, *how* that is to be done and what is required to do it. The economic struggle merely "impels" the workers to realized the government's attitude towards the working class. Consequently, *however much we may try* to "lend the economic, struggle itself a political character", *we shall never be able* to develop the political consciousness of the workers (to the level of Social-Democratic political consciousness) by keeping within the framework of the economic struggle, for *that framework is too narrow.* The Martynov formula has some value for us, not because it illustrates Martynov's aptitude for confusing things, but because it pointedly expresses the basic error that all the Economists commit, namely, their conviction that it is possible to develop the class political consciousness of the workers *from within*, so to speak, from their economic struggle, i.e., by making this struggle the exclusive (or, at least, the main) starting-point, by making it the exclusive (or, at least, the main) basis. Such a view is radically wrong. Piqued by our polemics against them, the Economists refuse to ponder deeply over the origins of these disagreements, with the result that we simply cannot understand one another. It is as if we spoke in different tongues. Class political consciousness can be brought to the workers *only from without,* only from outside the economic struggle, from outside the sphere of relations between workers and employers. The sphere from which alone it is possible to obtain this knowledge is the sphere of relationships of *all* classes and strata to the state and the government, the sphere of the interrelations between *all* classes. For that reason, the reply to the question as to what must be done to bring political knowledge to the workers cannot be merely the answer with which, in the majority of cases, the practical workers, especially those inclined towards Economism, mostly content themselves, namely: "To go among the workers." To bring political knowledge to the *workers* the Social Democrats must *go among all classes of the population*; they must dispatch units of their army *in all directions.*

We deliberately select this blunt formula, we deliberately express ourselves in this sharply simplified manner, not because we desire to indulge in paradoxes, but in order to "impel" the Economists to a realization of their tasks which they unpardonably ignore, to suggest to them strongly the difference between trade-unionist and Social-Democratic politics, which they refuse to understand. We therefore beg the reader not to get wrought up, but to hear us patiently to the end. Let us take the type of Social-Democratic study circle that has become most widespread in the past few years and examine its work. It has "contacts with the workers" and rests content with this, issuing leaflets in which abuses in the factories, the government's partiality towards the capitalists, and the tyranny of the police are strongly condemned. At workers' meetings the discussions never, or rarely ever, go beyond the limits of these subjects. Extremely rare are the lectures and discussions held on the history of the revolutionary movement, on questions of the government's home and foreign policy, on questions of the economic evolution of Russia and of Europe, on the position of the various classes in modern society, etc. As to systematically acquiring and extending contact with other classes of society, no one even dreams of that. In fact, the ideal leader, as the majority of the members of such circles picture him, is something far more in the nature of a trade union secretary than a socialist political leader. For the secretary of any, say English, trade union always helps the workers to carry on the economic struggle, he helps them to expose factory abuses, explains the injustice of the laws and of measures that hamper the freedom to strike and to picket (i. e., to warn all and sundry that a strike is proceeding at a certain factory), explains the partiality of arbitration court judges who belong to the bourgeois classes, etc., etc.

In a word, every trade union secretary conducts and helps to conduct "the economic struggle against the employers and the government". It cannot be too strongly maintained that *this is still not* Social-Democracy, that the Social-Democrat's ideal should not be the trade union secretary, but *the tribune of the people*, who is able to react to every manifestation of tyranny and oppression, no matter where it appears, no matter what stratum or class of the people it affects; who is able to generalize all these manifestations and produce a single picture of police violence and capitalist exploitation; who is able to take advantage of every event, however small, in order to set forth *before all* his socialist convictions and his democratic demands, in order to clarify for *all* and everyone the world-historic significance of the struggle for the emancipation of the proletariat. Compare, for example, a leader like Robert Knight (the well-known secretary and leader of the Boiler-Makers' Society, one of the most powerful trade unions in England), with Wilhelm Liebknecht, and try to apply to them the contrasts that Martynov draws in his controversy with *Iskra*.

Willielin Liebknecht engaged more in "the revolutionary elucidation of the whole of the present system or partial manifestations of it" (38-39); that Robert Knight "formulated the immediate demands of the proletariat and indicated the means by which they can be achieved" whereas Wilhelm Liebknecht, while doing this, did not hold back from "simultaneously guiding the activities of various opposition strata", "dictating a positive programme of action for them" Robert Knight strove "as far as possible to lend the economic struggle itself a political character" and was excellently able "to submit to the government concrete demands promising certain palpable results" whereas Liebknecht engaged to a much greater degree in "one-sided" "exposures" that Robert Knight attached more significance to the "forward march of the drab everyday struggle" whereas Liebknecht attached more significance to the "propaganda of brilliant and completed ideas" that Liebknecht converted the paper he was directing into "an organ of revolutionary opposition that exposed the state of affairs in our country, particularly the political state of affairs, insofar as it affected the interests of the most varied strata of the population" whereas Robert Knight "worked for the cause of the working class in close organic connection with the proletarian struggle" if by "close and organic connection" is meant the subservience to spontaneity which we examined above, by taking the examples of Krichevsky and Martynov – and "restricted the sphere of his influence", convinced, of course, as is Martynov, that "by doing so he deepened that influence".

Social Democrat, if he really believes it necessary to develop comprehensively the political consciousness of the proletariat, must "go among all classes of the population". This gives rise to the questions: how is this to be done? have we enough forces to do this? is there a basis for such work among all the other classes? will this not mean a retreat, or lead to a retreat, from the class point of view?

No one doubts that the theoretical work of Social-Democrats should aim at studying all the specific features of the social and political condition of the various classes. But extremely little is done in this direction as compared with the work that is done in studying the specific features of factory life. In the committees and study circles, one can meet people who are immersed in the study even of some special branch of the metal industry; but one can hardly ever find members of organisations (obliged, as often happens, for some reason or other to give up practical work) who are especially engaged in gathering material on some pressing question of social and political life in our country which could serve as a means for conducting Social-Democratic work among other strata of the population. In dwelling upon the fact that the majority of the present-day leaders of the working-class movement lack training, we cannot refrain from mentioning training in this respect also, for it too is bound up with the Economist conception of "close organic connection with the proletarian struggle". The principal thing, of course, is *propaganda* and *agitation* among all strata of the people. The work of the West European Social-Democrat is in this respect facilitated by the public meetings and rallies which *all* are free to attend, and by the fact that in parliament he addresses the representatives of *all* classes. We have neither a parliament nor freedom of assembly; nevertheless, we are able to arrange meetings of workers who desire to listen to *a Social-Democrat.*

They do not even understand that it is our task, the task of the progressive representatives of bourgeois democracy to lend the workers' economic struggle *itself* a political character. Why, we too, like the West-European bourgeois, want to draw the workers into politics, *but only into trade-unionist, not into Social-Democratic politics.* Trade-unionist politics of the working class is precisely *bourgeois politics* of the working class, and this 'vanguard's' formulation of its task is the formulation of trade-unionist politics.

The ideal audience for political exposure is the working class, which is first and foremost in need of all-round and live political knowledge, and is most capable of converting this knowledge into active struggle, even when that struggle does not promise "palpable results".

A tribune for *nation-wide* exposures can be only an all-Russia newspaper. "Without a political organ, a political movement deserving that name is inconceivable in the Europe of today"; in this respect Russia must undoubtedly be included in present-day Europe. The press long ago became a power in our country, otherwise the government would not spend tens of thousands of rubles to bribe it and to subsidize the Katkovs and Meshcherskys. And it is no novelty in autocratic Russia for the underground press to break through the wall of censorship and *compel* the legal and conservative press to speak openly of it. This was the case in the seventies and even in the fifties. How much broader and deeper are now the sections of the people willing to read the illegal underground press, and to learn from it "how to live and how to die"', to use the expression of a worker who sent a letter to *Iskra* (No. 7). Political exposures are as much a declaration of war against the *government* as economic exposures are a declaration of war against the factory owners. The moral significance of this declaration of war will be all the greater, the wider and more powerful the campaign of exposure will be and the more numerous and determined the social *class* that has *declared war in order to begin the war.* Hence, political exposures in themselves serve as a powerful instrument for *disintegrating* the system we oppose, as a means for diverting from the enemy his casual or temporary allies, as a means for spreading hostility and distrust among the permanent partners of the autocracy.

In our time only a party that will *organise* really *nation-wide* exposures can become the vanguard of the revolutionary forces. The word "nation-wide" has a very profound meaning.

The overwhelming majority of the non-working- class exposures (be it remembered that in order to become the vanguard, we must attract other classes) are sober politicians and level-headed men of affairs. They know perfectly well how dangerous it is to "complain" even against a minor official, let alone against the "omnipotent" Russian Government. And they will come *to us* with their complaints only when they see that these complaints can really have effect, and that we represent *a political force.* In order to become such a force in the eyes of outsiders, much persistent and stubborn work is required *to raise* our own consciousness, initiative, and energy.. To accomplish this it is not enough to attach a "vanguard" label to rearguard theory and practice.

Organisation of Workers and Organisation of Revolutionaries

It is only natural to expect that for a Social-Democrat whose conception of the political struggle coincides with the conception of the "economic struggle against the employers and the government", the "organisation of revolutionaries" will more or less coincide with the "organisation of workers". This, in fact, is what actually happens; so that when we speak of organisation, we literally speak in different tongues.

What was the source of our disagreement? It was the fact that on questions both of organization and of politics the Economists are forever lapsing from Social-Democracy into trade-unionism. The political struggle of Social-Democracy is far more extensive and complex than the economic struggle of the workers against the employers and the government. Similarly (indeed for that reason), the organisation of the revolutionary Social-Democratic Party must inevitably be of *a kind different* from the organisation of the workers designed for this struggle. The workers' organisation must in the first place be a trade union organisation; secondly, it must be as broad as possible; and thirdly, it must be as public as conditions will allow .

On the other hand, the organisation of the revolutionaries must consist first and foremost of people who make revolutionary activity their profession. In view of this common characteristic of the members of such an organisation, *all distinctions as between workers and intellectuals*, not to speak of distinctions of trade and profession, in both categories, *must be effaced*. Such an organisation must perforce not be very extensive and must be as secret as possible. Let us examine this threefold distinction. In countries where political liberty exists the distinction between a trade union and a political organisation is clear enough, as is the distinction between trade unions and Social Democracy. The relations between the latter and the former will naturally vary in each country according to historical, legal, and other conditions; they may be more or less close, complex, etc. (in our opinion they should be as close and as little complicated as possible); but there can be no question in free countries of the organisation of trade unions coinciding with the organisation of the Social-Democratic Party. In Russia, however, the yoke of the autocracy appears at first glance to obliterate all distinctions between the Social- Democratic organisation and the workers' associations, since *all* workers' associations and *all* study circles are prohibited, and since the principal manifestation and weapon of the workers' economic struggle – the strike – is regarded as a criminal (and sometimes even as a political!) offence. Conditions in our country, therefore, on the one hand, strongly" impel" the workers engaged in economic struggle to concern themselves with political questions, and, on the other, they "impel" Social-Democrats to confound trade-unionism with Social-Democracy (and our Krichevskys, Martynoys, and Co., while diligently discussing the first kind of "impulsion", fail to notice the second). Indeed, picture to yourselves people who are immersed ninety-nine per cent in "the economic struggle against the employers and the government". Some of them will never, during the *entire* course of their activity (from four to six months), be impelled to think of the need for a more complex organisation of revolutionaries. Others, perhaps, will come across the fairly widely distributed Bernsteinian literature, from which they will become convinced of the profound importance of the forward movement of "the drab everyday struggle". Still others will be carried away, perhaps, by the seductive idea of showing the world a new example of "close and organic contact with the proletarian struggle" – contact between the trade union and the Social Democratic movements. Such people may argue that the later a country enters the arena of capitalism and, consequently, of the working-class movement, the more the socialists in that country may take part in, and support, the trade union movement, and the less the reason for the existence of non-Social-Democratic trade unions. So far the argument is fully correct; unfortunately, however, some go beyond that and dream of a complete fusion of Social-Democracy with trade-unionism. We shall soon see, from the example of the Rules of the St. Petersburg League of Struggle, what a harmful effect such dreams have upon our plans of organisation.

The workers' organisations for the economic struggle should be trade union organisations. Every Social-Democratic worker should as far as possible assist and actively work in these organisations. But, while this is true, it is certainly not in our interest to demand that only Social-Democrats should be eligible for membership in the "trade" unions, since that would only narrow the scope of our influence upon the masses. Let every worker who understands the need to unite for the struggle against the employers and the government join the trade unions. The very aim of the trade unions would be impossible of achievement, if they did not unite all who have attained at least this elementary degree of understanding, if they were not very *broad* organisations. The broader these organisations, the broader will be our influence over them – an influence due, not only to the "spontaneous" development of the economic struggle, but to the direct and conscious effort of the socialist trade union members to influence their comrades. But a broad organisation cannot apply methods of strict secrecy (since this demands far greater training than is required for the economic struggle). How is the contradiction between the need for a large membership and the need for strictly secret methods to be reconciled? How are we to make the trade unions as public as possible? Generally speaking, there can be only two ways to this end: either the trade unions become legalised (in some countries this preceded the legalisation of the socialist and political unions), or the organisation is kept secret, but so "free" and amorphous, *lose* as the Germans say, that the need for secret methods becomes almost negligible as far as the bulk of the members is concerned.

The legalisation of non-socialist and non-political labour unions in Russia has begun and there is no doubt that every advance made by our rapidly growing Social-Democratic working-class movement will multiply and encourage attempts at legalisation – attempts proceeding for the most part from supporters of the existing order, but partly also from the workers themselves and from liberal intellectuals. The banner of legality has already been hoisted by the Vasilyevs and the Zubatovs. Support has been promised and rendered by the Ozerovs and the Wormses, and followers of the new tendency are now to be found among the workers. Henceforth, we cannot but reckon with this tendency. How we are to reckon with it, on this there can be no two opinions among Social-Democrats. We must steadfastly expose any part played in this movement by the Zubatovs and the Vasilyeys, the gendarmes and the priests, and explain their real intentions to the workers. We must also expose all the conciliatory, "harmonious" notes that will be heard in the speeches of liberal politicians at legal meetings of the workers, irrespective of whether the speeches are motivated by an earnest conviction of the desirability of peaceful class collaboration, by a desire to curry favor with the powers that be, or whether they are simply the result of clumsiness. Lastly, we must warn the workers against the traps often set by the police, who at such open meetings and permitted societies spy out the "fiery ones" and try to make use of legal organisations to plant their *agents provocateurs* in the illegal organisations.

Doing all this does not at all mean forgetting that *in the long* run the legalisation of the working-class movement will be, to our advantage, and not to that of the Zubatovs.

On the contrary, it is precisely our campaign of exposure that will help us to separate the tares from the wheat. What the tares are, we have already indicated. By the wheat we mean attracting the attention of ever larger numbers, including the most backward sections, of the workers to social and political questions, and freeing ourselves, the revolutionaries, from functions that are essentially legal (the distribution of legal books, mutual aid, etc.), the development of which will inevitably provide us with an increasing quantity of material for agitation.

Social-Democracy "executive groups" in relation to the economic struggle of the Workers.It would be difficult to show more glaringly how the Economists' ideas deviate from Social-Democracy to trade-unionism, and how alien to them is any idea that a Social-Democrat must concern himself first and foremost with an organization of revolutionaries capable of guiding the *entire* proletarian struggle for emancipation. To talk of "the political emancipation of the working class" and of the struggle against "tsarist despotism", and at the same time to draft rules like these, means to have no idea whatsoever of the real political tasks of Social-Democracy. But most characteristic, perhaps, is the amazing top-heaviness of the whole "system" which attempts to bind each single factory and its "committee" by a permanent string of uniform and ludicrously petty rules and a three-stage system of election. Hemmed in by the narrow outlook of Economism, the mind is lost in details that positively reek of red tape and bureaucracy. In practice, of course, three-fourths of the clauses are never applied; on the other hand, a "secret" organisation of this kind, with its central group in each factory, makes it very easy for the gendarmes to carry out raids on a vast scale. The Polish comrades have passed through a similar phase in their movement, with everybody enthusiastic about the extensive organisation of workers' benefit funds; but they very quickly abandoned this idea when they saw that such organisations only provided rich harvests for the gendarmes. If we have in mind broad workers' organisations, and not widespread arrests, if we do not want to provide satisfaction to the gendarmes, we must see to it that these organizations remain without any rigid formal structure. But will they be able to function in that case? Let us see what the functions are: To observe all that goes on in the factory and keep a record of events" . Do we really require a formally established group for this purpose? Could not the purpose be better served by correspondence conducted in the illegal papers without the setting up of special groups? " To lead the struggles of the workers for the improvement of their workshop conditions". This requires no set organisational form. Any sensible agitator can in the course of ordinary conversation gather what the demands of the workers are and transmit them to a narrow not a broad – organisation of revolutionaries for expression in a leaflet. "

It may be objected that an organisation which is so *lose* that it is not even definitely formed, and which has not even an enrolled and registered membership, cannot be called an organisation at all. Perhaps not the name is important. What is important is that this "organisation without members" shall do everything that is required, and from the very outset ensure a solid connection between our future trade unions and socialism. Only an incorrigible utopian would have a *broad* organisation of workers, with elections, reports, universal suffrage, etc., under the autocracy.

The moral to be drawn from this is simple. If we begin with the solid foundation of a strong organisation of revolutionaries, we can ensure the stability of the movement as a whole and carry out the aims both of Social-Democracy and of trade unions proper. If, we begin with a broad workers' organisation, which is supposedly most "accessible" to the masses (but which is actually most accessible to the gendarmes and makes revolutionaries most accessible to the police), we shall achieve neither the one aim nor the other; we shall not eliminate our rule-of-thumb methods, and, because we remain scattered and our forces are constantly broken up by the police, we shall only make trade unions of the Zubatov and Ozerov type the more accessible to the masses. What, properly speaking, should be the functions of the organisation of revolutionaries?

We shall deal with this question in detail. First, however, let us examine a very typical argument advanced by our terrorist, who (sad fate!) in this matter also is a next-door neighbour to the Economist. *Svoboda*, a journal published for workers, contains in its first issue an article entitled "Organisation", the author of which tries to defend his friends, the Economist workers of Ivanovo-Voznesensk. He wrote ;It is bad when the masses are mute and unenlightened, when the movement does not come from the rank and file. For instance, the students of a university town leave for their homes during the summer and other holidays, and immediately the workers' movement comes to a standstill. Can a workers' movement which has to be pushed on from outside be a real force? No, indeed.... It has not yet learned to walk, it is still in leading-strings. So it is in all matters. The students go off, and everything comes to a standstill. The most capable are seized; the cream is skimmed and the milk turns sour. If the 'committee' is arrested, everything comes to a standstill until a new one can he formed. And one never knows what sort of committee will be set up next it may be nothing like the former. The first said one thing, the second may say the very opposite. Continuity between yesterday and tomorrow is broken, the experience of the past does not serve as a guide for the future. The professional revolutionaries must and will make it our business to engage in *this kind* of "pushing on" a hundred times more forcibly than we have done hitherto. But the very fact that you select so hideous a phrase as "pushing on from outside" – a phrase which cannot but rouse in the workers (at least in the workers who are as unenlightened as you yourselves) a sense of distrust towards *all* who bring them political knowledge and revolutionary experience from outside, which cannot but rouse in them an instinctive desire to resist *all* such people – proves you to be demagogues, and *demagogues* are the worst enemies of the working class.

CHAPTER - VI

OBSERVATION AND CONCLUSION

Observation

The articulated point of labour transition and the labour movement in the 18th Century was bourgeois nature. The dynasty of Europe, France emperor's were ruled and administer with monarchy and Vested-Interest domination. The policy and ruling atmosphere where suitable for day to day life of "ordinary Citizens" there may be a peasant or peaceful life. This consideration is a limitation by which acute freedom. The situation might have changed , the entire administrative set up has devastated due to the milieu of the emperors mind set and bias with peer groups and pressure of contemporaries. Therefore, the structure of life pattern and an entire corner of the General public (ordinary citizens) were trapped by the emperor's atmosphere. The realistic approach or idealistic thought which is referred by 'Sacra *tees'* was very meager level.

However, the issues or complicated thought for human being approach were 'constant' in terms of utilization by haves and have not. These are the major reasons for literature (poet, writers, dramatist) the concept of labour in the sense of performance with sensitized approach i.e. related to social class, ethical attachment, racial, the position in which royal life (person who performed the service under the duke, queen) actually it was one kind of slaveries done by dictators. They (service provider) thought themselves as a supreme for their followers (next phase category of the society). Therefore, most of the criticism, quoted point was the nature or elements of lifestyle measured by labour are dependency with economic value and social value.

The highlighted by writers, poets and dramatist have generalized the human being associated factors were reflected and expression of opinion. They are philanthropic approach, generosity of mind, range of life style, dedication, contribution. According to their criticism, social value was neglected by the capitalist. Whereas, desire by poor class or working class were hidden from the trial. Because of the initial stage they followed the cruel method. They vanished by bourgeois or total civil society. The purpose or acute demand for fulfillment of the personal desire. They (labour category either freedom of life or slavery) followed or mingled with them as well as performed whatever that directed, command (capitalist) as a result minimum number of people only benefited and majority of them suffered such kind of practices. It was a miracle of historical event and literature antecedent in which fitness of poor class and working class life.

Conclusion

The combined literature (English writers, dramatist) sources were described about the phenomena of "labour" is a service provider to supreme value persons in the society in the early 18th century and after the 18th century. During the emperors rule the laborers customs on family concern, cultural fitness, mingle with equal civilized manners were restricted by high class people. After intervention by Karl Marx, the imperialism and dictatorship approach were gradually eliminated through large amounts of agitation by various crusaders at the time of industrial, French revolution. Hence this period was called golden days of labors renaissance.

After the 19th century, the nature and significance of the labour movement were pushed into capitalistic movement without any kind of in flittered activities in the society. In contrary, pull-factor leads to the labour category who involved with the corporate sector (capitalist movement) forsaking of desire with modernized living culture. They are not bothering about unfair working condition and ill-treat or discriminate by capitalist in this era.

References

1. Allett J. *"New Liberalism: the Political Economy of J. A. Hobson"*, University of Toronto Press. 1981.

2. Amin S. *"Imperialism and Unequal Development"*, Hassocks: Harvester Press, and New York: Monthly Review Press; first published in French, 1977.

3. Amin S. *"Class and Nation: Historically and in the Present Crisis"*, New York: Monthly Review Press; first published in French, 1980.

4. Arrighi G. *"International corporations, labour aristocracies and economic development in tropical Africa"*, Rhodes, 1970.

5. Aston T. H. and Philpin C.H.E. (eds) *"The Brenner Debate: Agrarian Class Structure and Economic Development in Pre-Industrial Europe"*, Cambridge University Press, 1985.

6. Barone C. "Samir Amin and the theory of imperialism: a critical analysis", *Review of Radical Political Economics,* Vol. 14, 1982.

7. Braverman H. *"Labor and Monopoly Capital"*, New York: Monthly Review Press, 1974.

8. Brewer A. *"Marxist Theories of Imperialism: a Critical Survey"*, first edn, London: Routledge & Kegan Paul, 1980b.

9. Brewer A. "Trade with fixed real wages and mobile capital", *Journal of International Economics,* Vol. 18, 1985.

10. Bayley J. "Oliver Twist: 'Things as They Are'", John Gross, Gabriel Pearson, eds., *Dickens and the Twentieth Century*, Toronto: University of Toronto Press, 1962.

11. Cazamian L. *The Social Novel in England, 1830-1850: Dickens, Disraeli, Mrs. Gaskell, Kingsley.*1903. Translated by Martin Fido. London: Routlege & Kegan Paul, 1973.

12. Cain P. J., "J. A. Hobson, Cobdenism, and the radical theory of economic imperialism", *Economic History Review,* 31, 1978.

13. Dobb M. *"Political Economy and Capitalism"*, 2nd edn, London: Routledge & Kegan Paul, first edn published 1937, 1940.

14. Dumont R. and Mazoyer M. *"Socialisms and Development"*, London: Deutsch; first published in French 1969, 1973.

15. Etherington N. *"Theories of Imperialism: War, Conquest and Capital"*, Beckenham, Kent: Croom Helm, 1984.

16. Foster-Carter A. *"Marxism vs. Dependency Theory? A Polemic"*, University of Leeds, Department of Sociology, Occasional Paper no. 8, 1979.

17. Friedman A.L. *"Industry and Labour"*, London: Macmillan, 1977.

18. Gibson B. "Unequal exchange; theoretical issues and empirical findings", *Review of Radical Political Economics,* Vol. 12, 1980.

19. Harrison and John R. Harrison, "Dickens's Literary Architecture: Patterns of Ideas and Imagery", *Hard Times. Papers on Language & Literature, Southern Illinois University,* Vol. 36, 2000.

20. James L. "The Nineteenth Social-Novel in England", *Encyclopedia of Literature and Criticism*, ed. by John Peck. London: Routledge, 1990.

21. Joel Mokyr (1994) 'Technological Change, 1700-1830', in R Floud and D McCloskey, eds., The Economic History of Britain since 1700 (Cambridge, 2nd edn. 1994), Pp. 13. Mokyr, Lever of Riches, Pp. 82.

22. De Vries J. "The industrial revolution and the industrious revolution", Journal of Economic History, Vol. 54, 1994.

23. Laclau E. (1971) "Feudalism and capitalism in Latin America", *New Left Review,* May/June; reprinted, with postscript, in Laclau (1977).

24. Maxine Berg. "*Age of Manufactures, 1700-1820*". Industry, Innovation and Work in Britain, London, 2nd edn., 1994.

25. Miles R. "*Capitalism and Unfree Labour: Anomaly or Necessity?*", London: Tavistock, 1987.

26. Crafts N.F.R. "*British Economic Growth during the Industrial Revolution*", Oxford, 1985.

27. Idem, "*British economic growth, 1700-1831: a review*", Economic History Review.

28. Owen R. and Sutcliffe B. (eds) "*Studies in the Theory of Imperialism*", London: Longman, 1972.

29. Porter B. "*Critics of Empire; British Radical Attitudes to Colonialism in Africa, 1895-1914*", London: Macmillan, 1968.

30. Sutcliffe B. "*Imperialism and industrialisation in the Third World*", Owen and Sutcliffe, 1972.

31. Sweezy P. "*The Theory of Capitalist Development*", New York: Oxford University Press, 1942.

www.ingramcontent.com/pod-product-compliance
Lightning Source LLC
LaVergne TN
LVHW051300200726

843510LV00010B/1216